PRAISE FOR *SISTERHOOD ECONOMY*

'*Sisterhood Economy* isn't just a book of despair. It is one of hope—which springs, as it should, from women's own accounts.' BUSINESS STANDARD

'Shaili Chopra tells untold stories about common women from different walks of life in an empathetic, non-judgmental tone—thus forming the bedrock for substantial change.' MILLENNIUM POST

'*Sisterhood Economy* reveals the challenges that the modern Indian woman has to face—both at home and in the workplace—and how she can overcome them. The author champions the cause of ordinary women.' THE TELEGRAPH

'This book brings us an understanding, an empathy, a deep sorrow, and a sense of anger on what all women have to put up with, even as it instils a fierce pride at how we are managing to forge ahead, break free of conventions. It's a book that not only all women should read, but also all men.' HINDU BUSINESS LINE

'Shaili touches upon the most relevant issues of our times which most often are closed door conversations in a highly readable, heroic and engaging way... bringing a powerful, authentic and honest lens to women and the economy.' MASABA GUPTA

'A powerful book with many anecdotes of everyday women encountering and defeating the patriarchy, *Sisterhood Economy* will fill you with optimism and hope.' FAYE D'SOUZA

'Shaili Chopra has a chatty and engrossing style of writing... Mainstreaming of sisterhood is not just about the economy, it is also about the society India desires.' BIBEK DEBROY

'*Sisterhood Economy* by Shaili Chopra is important, apt and timely. It brings to you real-life stories of the barriers women face as contributors to the economy... we are the real wealth creators and yet very little recognition of the existing barriers are discussed or resolved.' PRIYANKA CHATURVEDI

'When women rise, they lift up society. *Sisterhood Economy* is a deeply reflective book that explores and narrates the power of equitable ground for women.' FALGUNI NAYAR

Sisterhood Economy

Sisterhood Economy

Of, By, For Wo(men)

SHAILI CHOPRA

SIMON &
SCHUSTER

London · New York · Sydney · Toronto · New Delhi

First published in India by Simon & Schuster India, 2022

1 3 5 7 9 10 8 6 4 2

Simon & Schuster India
818, Indraprakash Building,
21, Barakhamba Road,
New Delhi 110001
www.simonandschuster.co.in

PB ISBN: 978-81-972789-9-0
eBook ISBN: 978-93-92099-14-4

Simon & Schuster: Celebrating 100 Years of Publishing in 2024

Typeset in India by SÜRYA, New Delhi

Printed and bound in India by Replika Press Pvt. Ltd.

Contents

For Abeer and Bani

Introduction

When I left the television studio to become an entrepreneur, nearly everyone I knew thought I had really lost my mind to quit a job that put me in front of global audiences, to one of hiding. I got calls from all my friends—journalists, bankers, politicians, CEOs, well-wishers, family—asking me "Who retires at 30? From being a national TV anchor?"

I wanted to tell stories that I couldn't find around me. Stories of women. But no one understood why that was "a plan". "What a niche you have chosen," said one. At approximately 50% of a country's population, women were being called a "segment" and that just didn't go down well for me. It's like we are willing to ignore one half of our talent because it didn't wear a black suit?

Somehow, the inspiration came in a weird package and triggered change inside me in 2011. I landed on the early flight into Bangalore. This was an interview I had always wanted to do. Warren Buffett was on his first trip to India and I, a primetime television journalist, wanted to make a real impression on him. As a woman covering business news, CEOs, and the next big deal,

Buffett perhaps epitomised the prize among interviews as it were. He spoke about all the right things and I asked all the tough questions. But I came back asking myself if I was made to just interview the rich and famous. I mean, this was it. I was telling stories of those who had made it. Something about doing that interview switched a button inside me. Where were the people who hadn't made it? Buffett was the 276th man I had interviewed. Where were the women?

It was a weird moment because journalists go from stories and interviews to their next big ones. And here I was, feeling bereft of inspiration and ideas of being in this moment in journalism. So, I literally stood up in the newsroom and asked—aren't we bored of stories of the same guys making it bigger and bigger every single day?

Many bobbed their heads and gave me an awkward smile, but my message box poured over with yeses. And so I put in my papers and my resignation read two words: "am off".

Like many other women on earth, my head was bustling with self-doubt and questions as I set course on something new. This was 2012. I had no idea what I was going to build or how. But I knew it would be about women. I took a little smartphone and went around interviewing young, old, quiet, loud, meek, confident, charming, unsure women from all walks of life. "What have I done to be interviewed?" nearly every woman said, with a side of guilt and self-doubt.

Aren't we conditioned to do that? I couldn't possibly start a revolution alone. Or could I? Our worlds were shaped by a narrative that went mostly like the films we watch. There's always the hero who rescued the woman and changed her future. At home, you could either have an opinion or a good relationship with your parents. At college it was 'so amaze' that your parents even 'let you study' for a masters. Discussing money was blasphemous because money would give women the choice of leaving loveless, abusive marriages. There was a world order and shaking it couldn't be a woman's job. Because it was already prescribed and disruptors aren't anyone's favourites.

In the course of my interviews, I met women from everywhere. Malti was a housemaid who worked three homes and ran her household after her husband—a mill worker in Mumbai—decided to give up on working at 29 to live off her earnings. Noor, 33, was shortchanged in marriage because she was forced to fund her husband's drunken nights. Prabha, 41, was leading a private equity firm but entirely invisible because "it pays to have guys on your team and not be the face of it". Tripti, 26, had had twins and was judged for returning to work in ten days because she "wanted to work while the babies slept, what else was there to do anyway?" Simran, 25, got her husband to join her business because "raising money" was not possible for her alone.

In 2012, a young girl was gruesomely raped in India. It changed many of us. It completely broke me down. Rape wasn't a woman's issue, it was a national concern. It took the media that severe a case, and one that occured in the heart of the capital rather than the forgotten towns and villages of our country, to put women's issues on the front pages. This needed to change.

We talk about how many women were raped, not about how many men raped women. We talk of how many girls were harassed, but not about how many boys harass girls. We talk of violence against women, we forget to mention who it is perpetrated by and how it's something "against" women.

With all these in my recesses, I took a leap of faith and started a platform for women, *SheThePeople*, seven years ago. Yet I felt I needed to justify it. I spent days and hours explaining to people (including women) why women needed a platform of their own, a safe space to discuss life, work, insecurities, and more. Women need to stop justifying themselves. But even I did. It was so deep-rooted.

I used basic math and picked numbers to drive my inspiration. Indian women are almost 50% of India's population. As a ratio of the world's population, that is 9%. To give you an idea, women in India are three times the size of Brazil, five times the size of Japan and twice the size of the United States of America. We women are not a number, we are a force. And not enough people are telling us this. We aren't telling ourselves this enough.

Here's something to think about. We are not just half of the population. We produce and raise the other half. We are half the vote in our country. So we should be at least half the voice. But we are not. Why are we absent from the headlines? Why don't we know the amazing stories of so many women? Why do only one in five women work? That's what I wanted to get behind.

As I started work on this book, *The Sisterhood*

Economy, COVID-19 had hit us right in the face. The impacts of crises are never gender-neutral, and COVID-19 was no exception. As quarantine measures keep people at home, close schools and day-care facilities, the burden* of unpaid care and domestic work has exploded. Both for women and men. But even before COVID-19, women spent an average of 4.1 hours per day performing unpaid work, while men spent 1.7 hours—that means women did three times more unpaid care work than men, worldwide.

The pandemic saw urban Indian men spending more time in the kitchen. It was an eye-opener for many in terms of the quantum of chores that needed to be done when you stay at home. While women have been owning the workspaces too, it was time men show the same gesture at home. We need to get rid of the stereotype that men can earn well but not cook while women can cook well but not earn. Earning and cooking are basic survival skills. But as COVID-19 restrictions wore off, women got back to status quo, and most men who experimented with household chores let them remain on Instagram timelines and no more.

Women's issues are everyone's problems. In fact, we also need to think of women outside of their problems and celebrate their achievements. Big, small, tiny—all of them. Another inspiration for me to tell stories about women was how we have for years reduced them to those who "needed to be empowered" giving the other side some sort of unwritten responsibility to

*https://www.unwomen.org/en/news/stories/2020/9/feature-covid-19-economic-impacts-on-women

"fix" things for women. I don't think someone else has to give women power. They have it, we just enable them to discover it.

How can a country progress if nearly half its population is not working? As an economics student, I asked myself—what holds us back from recognising that women are a big (and absent) source of progress and outcomes?

This book brings together stories of women and their changing realities. Women talk about themselves, and their journeys through workplaces, within families, through singlehood, divorce, successes, through feelings of loneliness, sexual pleasure, breakdown, rising up, and more. Through the many chapters, it asks some fundamental questions.

When will science stop treating women as walking wombs, baby machines and incubators of new life? When will films stop showing us as the damsel in distress? How will I learn to say no? When will women start living for themselves and not for others?

In chapters like Beauty Parlour Economics, to the Saasu Ma's Curse, you will hear women finding the guts from the very bottom of their circumstance and those who are paving the way for others to dream and run more easily. The many stories touch upon the lives of Puja from Deira-on-Sone and her escape to an urban city for agency and opportunity to Ketaki, a Mumbai-based triathlon runner, who literally woke up one morning to say she would live her life for herself and found how the universe moved things for her to succeed.

The Indian constitution starts with three words.

WeThePeople. But somewhere in the promise of justice and equality we forgot women. It's exactly that, *SheThePeople*, which I focus on, in this book. Just how can women build a sisterhood to support, understand with a judgement-free attitude towards each other, lifting themselves and others to the next level. Sometimes all it takes is the girl sitting on the next chair in the airport waiting lounge.

As per consulting firm McKinsey, the country could add up to $770 billion—more than 18%—to its GDP by 2025, simply by giving equal opportunities to women.

Part of the reason we are light years away from bridging the gender gap at work is how we portray women in media and public spaces, how we think of women in society as those "meant" to perform only specific roles, and the absence of a central and national-scale dialogue of how girls and women can contribute to the economy in an impactful way.

A 2016 survey shows, of every 1,000 stories done in the Indian media, 80% are on the Indian government, cricket and Bollywood. Women's social issues like entrepreneurship, abortion, child marriage, and others, collectively get only 10% of coverage.

For India to tap the latent potential of its women, we need to fix these anomalies. Fortunately, we have the opportunity to make quick changes and change equations thanks to digital inclusion and technology.

Here's a story I talk about later in the book. Rohini is a well-educated girl from western India, in Maharashtra's Satara district. Having completed her Masters in Arts, her parents were worried she was too qualified, too educated for anyone to marry her. When

Rohini did get married, her husband would not allow her to work even though she wanted to and had the requisite qualifications. Realising this, she enrolled in a learning course (which is a long route for women to escape the shackles of a home) and she opted for internet and computer learning. Rohini quickly figured the internet had many answers for her, from knowledge to opportunities. "So when my husband found a job in the city, I stayed back in the village and through the internet started doing odd jobs, one of which was beekeeping." Her village benefitted from her beekeeping, the society accepted her venture, and soon enough, Rohini started making honey and selling it via social media and other messaging apps. Her first batch was 10 bottles, her second was 50 and sold out before they were ready and her third was 500 bottles, branded and labelled. All done in a small room of her house by learning on the internet. Rohini had the fire to inspire so many of us.

The big question in my mind was always—why didn't I hear Rohini's story on the front pages of the newspaper? Why was no one talking about Rohini's ability to stand up for herself, launch a little venture and find financial independence? Our obsession as a country with a billion-dollar valuation was killing such sexy success stories.

When farmers in India die by suicide, the focus of both the government and the media starts and ends with the reasons of their death. What we forget to report on are the women and families they leave behind. Outside of the compensation announced, we seldom talk about or assess the economic impact on them.

A gendered lens, if mainstreamed into policy-making, and civil society efforts, will deeply improve possibilities for women and how a nation views them.

Like many other big decisions, efforts outside of the government also matter a lot. Many mini revolutions are taking place. Women know they deserve and need a spotlight on what they are doing, and why. Ours is a live struggle. It won't change until we talk about ourselves. We need to take on the status quo, the patriarchy, the policies, the politics. We can do this with flags and marches and we also bring change by telling stories. By having a conversation. Or writing books like this one.

So the key is this. As we move into the future, we need to think about what we are willing to accept. No constitution calls for inequality, but society does. Why should we be told what we are "allowed"? The question is, are you going to wait for change or go out and find it yourself?

It finally comes down to one powerful thought: Every woman just needed one person to not give up on her. And that was herself.

chapter one

The Women's Economy

How can India catapult into a superpower? Simply by treating its women better. It sounds like the switch of a button should make that possible, but we are a few decades, if not a century away, from creating fairer economic opportunities and a safe progressive society for women in India. For all these years, we have prioritised seemingly more important issues like poverty, hunger, and education, forgetting that putting women at the centre of all efforts could solve a cross section of national challenges. As a result, the story of India's women is the story of continuous change and contradictions.

When I started writing this book, there were three kinds of people I met. One who squarely dissed the idea that women could drive, lead, and grow economies. The second were those for whom women's issues made for the perfect cocktail party discussions, helping them gin-wash their efforts for women "empowerment". Daughters or daughters-in-law of big businessmen managed a small project focussed on women and somehow that became the token contribution of a large company towards the women's economy. The third set of people gave me hope and enough trigger to write this book. They were men and women who believed in building equal organisations, and spent time scaling up knowledge and efforts to change mindsets around, and including, more women at the workplace, at the policy tables, in the government and at home.

The women's economy offers us a measurable change. By encouraging more women to have jobs, careers, start-ups, small or big businesses, we can lift the financial status not just of women but also of their communities, their villages, their children, and families at large. This is a statistic I repeat many times in this book, only as a reminder of the potential women have in changing the status of a country. As per McKinsey, the country could add up to $770 billion—more than 18%—to its GDP by 2025, simply by giving equal opportunities to women.

Current estimates place India's rate of female participation in the formal labour force at only 24%—among the lowest in developing nations. What's worse, this figure isn't improving as more women get educated and become aware of the benefits of economic independence and financial freedom. The majority of Indian women work in the informal sector in jobs with limited social protection and low wages.

Growing up, cultural barriers and occupational segregation play important roles in limiting women's economic potential. As career aspirants, before women can dream, they are told to drop male-dominated career options, or pick those careers where they will flourish but also complete female-oriented familial responsibilities. At the workplace too, women in India tend to be grouped into industries and occupations that have not seen employment or wage growth in recent years.

While the women's economy will eventually become measurable, what remains very ambiguous and complex is the way our societies are designed. When you are a woman, it's a given that you will exist to meet expectations and a great deal will be already laid out for you to "fit in to".

"When I was growing up, my parents wanted me to join the Indian Administrative Services. Like most Indian girls, I heard my parents, who were more aware of what I should be doing than I was," says 24-year-old Radhika Singhal. "So, I opted to go into engineering and later prepare for the cut-throat civil services exam." Kumar didn't make it, she took up an odd job servicing marketing clients in an agency. One day, she got an offer to start out as a junior social media manager and took it merely because it paid well. "My salary check was bigger than most my age at 21. But social media made no sense to my parents. I, on the other hand, loved it. It gave me a great outlet to be the person I never knew I was. Soon came Tiktok and Instareels, and I was a celebrity. People loved me." But Kumar's parents were ready with their next salvo. With no "real" job in hand, they asked her to either opt for a more lady-like job, like a front-office or public relations position, or simply get married. "In either case, my online personality became an issue. I wasn't the homely girl who had a teaching job and returned home by 5 PM for family duties."

Rati Gupta, 25, is doing her PhD in English. For her, it's a way to push marriage back. For her parents it's a case of fattening the turkey for the final feast. "They think a well-educated girl will attract a better groom." The feminine urge to enrol in courses just to delay the societal urgency of getting married is real. Perhaps this explains why in India, like in many Asian countries, 42% of graduates are female but only 29% of entry-level professionals are female.

Things don't always change when you become successful and grow. The societal control over one's gender is so significant, it catches up along the way. And so, this journey is similar for everyone who makes it to the top. Two decades ago, when Pepsi CEO Indra Nooyi got her pivotal promotion, her mother cut off the announcement and sent her out to get milk instead. By restricting how women should work, we are slicing off the pie they can contribute to.

Even as India and its people-fabric changes, more and more women are now visible as scientists, business leaders, politicians, administrative officers, and more. We are celebrating our women more than ever before. But outside of that new-found glaze is a ground reality, in society, within families, and in every field—that women should only be "allowed" that much. This is linked to what women are expected to do.

A few years ago, I was talking to a male cousin who hadn't married until 47. In India, even men don't often have the luxury to stay single that long. But his reasons for not finding the right girl left me amused. "I want a woman who is modern and traditional at the same time." Puzzled, I probed him about his statement about what were the traits of such a person. "She should be a working woman, who drinks, who earns for herself, wears international clothes, but she should also be traditional, not raise her voice and keep the family together with good values." This really hit home an important point for me—India had a long way to go as far as women's equal rights and opportunities were concerned and that we were still living in some illusion about what a perfect woman should be.

What Does it Mean to Be a Woman in the Indian Economy Today?

Almost every woman is a working woman, only some are salaried. This should strike each one of us but doesn't. In the formal working sector, women have been working steadily and silently to contribute to economic growth and prosperity. Both in rural and urban India, they have ventured into the market with big and small initiatives to prove that they are as adept and intuitive about running businesses as men. At home, women are finally—thanks to breakthrough films, more media spotlight, and bigger headline communication by the government—beginning to hear and talk about the role women play at home, even when they are not employed outside.

This exposure has also reached India's rural belt, slowly but surely. Across India's villages, women entrepreneurs are willingly forging their own path, learning the internet and proving to be capable leaders for future generations. This is happening despite structural exclusion from the socio-economic hierarchy of their families and the immense psychological pressure levied on them.

Twenty-year-old Pragya Ganesh Lohan in Raigad is the district's first woman carpenter and together with her dad, the two are forcing the town's society to think progressively about working women. She learnt carpentry to take over her dad's business and dreams of opening a store. With training and new skills, she is contributing to the household's financial income and shutting down doubters over "girls can't do this". She was 16-years-old when she started accompanying her father, 45, to the workshop and learnt making metal and glass doors and windows by watching him. A female carpenter? Most people in the village were skeptical initially but now most people come and talk to her for their needs.

In an interview, she said that her father had been running the business for over a decade when he started looking for a partner. He asked her if she would join him and she was delighted. "I couldn't believe it."

Women are seeking opportunities against all odds. Shweta Katti grew up in a Mumbai brothel and went on to receive a full scholarship from New York's Bard College. Katti is a reminder of no dream being too big.

"I grew up in Mumbai's largest red light district, Kamathipura. Education and a safe environment were a huge struggle for me growing up," she writes of her journey.

Katti faced many hardships through her childhood in order to pursue education. She was supported by her mother, a sex worker, and a local NGO, who helped her continue her studies.

A social shift is also happening in a different way. For years, in India, we have seen a phenomenon where a large number of women who are educated were expected to sit at home with decorated degrees to their credit and not work. This was largely because many of India's rich believed their daughters must get educated from the best institutions but didn't "need to work" because they had a lot of family money. "My parents sent me to London School of Economics, but the day I landed, they showed me a boy and married me off," says a Kolkata-based entrepreneur who spent her time raising her children and attending kitty parties, because "what else could one do?" But now, girls from traditional business families from some communities are opening their own businesses to establish an identity for themselves. Sometimes helped by the men in their lives.

"I've been with a multinational for the last six years. Last year, I got the opportunity to move to America because we were expanding our team there and without even thinking twice, my husband said, 'You should definitely consider it.' Not even once did he say that, 'Oh! You're gonna move to America.' It was always WE.

"The funny thing, is we were just dating back then. But stars aligned and I got the job in America. We knew we were in love and wanted to spend the rest of our lives together, so we ended up planning the whole wedding in just three weeks. After we got married we stayed in India for six months because we wanted to spend time at home, before we made the move to Colorado.

"My husband is a software engineer. He was in a very good position in his company but he didn't even blink when it came to quitting his job to move with me and said 'I'll figure it out when we're there.' It was as if he cut off his wings just so I could fly and I will never stop being grateful for that. Even now, if I come back home after a tiring day at work, he makes me a meal from scratch and gets everything done.

"Our marriage is an equal partnership. We take all the important decisions together. Be it financials or household chores; we don't have gender roles in our relationship. We both do carpenter work and kitchen work together and that's the beauty of our relationship." While it is wonderful how supportive her husband has been and she is so grateful for it, there should also come a time in the future when women can take this sort of support for granted, just as men always have.

It's not money that women are after (though that is a perfectly legitimate goal) but it's the independence and self-confidence it brings them. "My money is my money," says Ruchi Pradhan, who has been setting up small businesses over the last decade. And so from rethinking a banarasi saree to making artisanal millet flour, women are driving change for themselves in a new India that's embracing technology at a breakneck speed. Nearly a billion Indians will have the internet by 2025.

While all of this change was underway, the world was hit by a pandemic that by some estimates has pushed the efforts of gender equality back by a generation. Women who had fought in every way to start a new chapter in their lives—by starting up—were faced with losses, business closure, and even debt. What this simply meant is that women needed to go back to being at the mercy of men, risk domestic violence and abuse, and have little independence in financial matters. One reason for this greater effect on women is that the pandemic significantly increased the burden of unpaid care, which at any given time is disproportionately carried by women. This, among other factors, means that women's employment is dropping faster than average, even accounting for the fact that women and men work in different sectors.

It's a basic principle of fairness: same education, same work, and same pay should be a reasonable expectation. Despite all the economic growth and the progress in gender conversations, the gap between what men and women are paid has not quite come down. At last check, it would take 257[*] years before the world could erase the pay imbalance between men and women.

Rewiring How Women Think of "Opportunities"

We have begun the debate on what constitutes unpaid work and how housework is work too but is just not paid for. But women and economists are both struggling to understand how this unpaid labour can be measured. The pandemic showed many unhelpful partners in a household, a small trailer of what unpaid

*https://www.nbcnews.com/news/world/it-will-be-257-years-women-have-equal-pay-new-n1103481

labour looks like. Outside of the celebratory selfies of men washing dishes and mopping the floors of their own homes, there is clearly a need for a deep and detailed conversation on how we can value a woman as a homemaker and create a more shared economy.

Part of this change will need women to rewire their thinking from being the sacrificial mothers, wives, and sisters, to those who stand ground on equal contribution. The change will not just come from policies and institutional efforts but from within.

"I have always been a homemaker. We were never raised to have dreams or jobs," says 61-year-old Kusum Kapur, married to an army general. "It's only now when my husband has retired and my children are married, did I find time to express a desire to run a small jute-bags business." Her daughter, Prakriti, 27, is married with two children who go to childcare while she works at a bank. "From the day I grew up, I knew I had to work and build my career and make my own money." It was not easy. Sending children to daycare is not considered normal in India, where extended families are expected to look after them or a well-structured nanny-cum-maid system is in place. "Your daughter-in-law is too busy to look after her little children," were the jibes Prakriti would overhear at family weddings. "Initially my in-laws were also cagey but have adjusted over time. My husband supported me and I consider that a big plus."

That women have to call themselves lucky to have partners who support or in-laws who "allow" them to work is a reflection of how hardwired women are about their position in the world. A recent Instagram post that went viral said, "Ambitious women really have only two options. A super supportive partner or no partner at all." This is also why women undersell themselves in the job market.

Women fish for low-paying jobs while men aim for high-paid jobs. Women are encouraged to take jobs that will help them "balance work and life" and not take up, say, a coder or a manager's job which may be more lucrative and have different timings. Given India has a dwindling female workforce, down to under 30%, this has only made things worse. Simply put, it means the more educated and aware women in India are getting, they are taking up less challenging jobs.

Why do women settle for less? Fundamentally, there are enough historical reasons for this.

Dharini Pandey's shocking story reminds you how blatant this conditioning is. Growing up, many women would probably tell you that society has often tried to shove the idea into their heads that no matter how successful they'd like to become when they're older, they probably never will earn as much as their male counterparts. When she joined a media house in Mumbai, with over 18 years of experience, her first meeting with the boss went a bit like this. "It's good to have poached you from another channel but please focus on putting your pretty face on the tele and don't think of running this channel or becoming the editor here. That cabin is only reserved for people like me." Pandey, a fearless television anchor, was stumped with this conversation and left the room with many questions in her head. "Was I not good enough? Maybe it's something that comes with age, I told myself. Maybe I needed to be better." She was so sure the problem lay with her. "Through my career, my bosses, all of whom were male, were quick to remind me I was growing 'too fast'. And that promotion came with time." It was only years later that Pandey realised that for men the promotions came when they displayed efficiencies or brought in big interviews and for women, "a process" and "time" had to determine that.

Is this because men are the traditional breadwinners and women supposedly aren't? There are many factors behind the wage, promotion, and position disparity between men and women.

It is disturbing that women and girls are internalising the gender pay gap and are looking for low-paid jobs themselves. They assume that they can never compete with men and so they settle for low-paying jobs. Puja Kumari, a game developer in Bangalore, says, "It is disappointing that women themselves are looking for low-paid jobs. If women internalise their discrimination in the economic field, how will we move forward?"

Another factor at play can be that women choose different occupations from men. Around the world, occupations like teachers pay less than occupations like engineers or coders. So gender differences in occupational choice affect gender differences in earnings.

Women Internalise That They Are Less than Men Both Professionally and Academically

A BBC report* says that the problem starts with the subject choice during higher studies. Women have

*https://www.bbc.co.uk/news/education-41693230

internalised the idea that men and women have inherently different academic and professional abilities. This is the reason why many women take up low-paying subjects like arts, home science, and humanities and not high paying subjects like computer science, engineering or science.

As per a study, women make up only 26% of the workforce in STEM which provides one of the highest-paying jobs. Women are afraid that they won't be able to compete with men in these fields since men are assumed to be naturally brilliant in STEM. Moreover, women also want to keep themselves away from the gender discrimination that is prevalent in this field. "I find that a lot of male scientists in India are completely insensitive to their female colleagues and are frequently dismissive of them," says Deepa Subramanyam,* stem cell biologist, in an interview.

Additionally for women, many of these high-paying jobs have been traditionally male dominated with hardly any inspiration for them to apply or join. In India too there is a persistent gender gap at higher ranks of management and leadership which is populated by a handful of self-made women, and a large number of puppet positions filled by women from within a businessman's family.

Having built *SheThePeople* all these years, another key insight into why women don't pick a high-paying job is—it's not because they don't know coding or maths or business, it's because women lack female

---

*https://www.shethepeople.tv/home-top-video/deepa-subramanyam-stem-cell-biologist-interview/

role models in these sectors. Women need to hear from other women how they navigate complex spaces where suited men lead and often question the calibre of female leaders. Role models and their storytelling and media coverage is one critical link to the change we are seeking in gender equality. You see it, you believe it.

How Marriage Affects Women's Decision to Seek Less-paid Jobs

Women have also accepted and internalised that they ultimately have to shift to part-time jobs or leave the labour force after marriage and so, they choose low-paying jobs. Studies have shown that after marriage or pregnancy, many women quit the workforce under the pressure to juggle both work and housework. Even if some women try to seek high-paid jobs, they drop it with the fear that earning more than a husband might be an invitation to taunts, disrespect and even abuse. Because it is not a hidden fact that the male ego is dented if the wife earns more.

Anu Abhivyakti, who lives in Gurgaon and works in the same company as her husband, says she declined a promotion because her husband didn't get his. "I literally prayed that I shouldn't get promoted. After years I regret that, but I didn't want our work to break our family." Indian men in particular have been raised on a diet of expectations from a woman and all the gendered roles she will perform. One of those is how often she will sacrifice what's hers for her family or husband. "Our parents educate us, but we as women fail ourselves often in this journey to compromise," rues Acharya, who worked in a global tech outsourcing firm.

It's not just promotions. It's parenthood sacrifice too that women internalise.

The "Family" Factor

"A parenthood premium for the men. And a parenthood penalty for the women. This is really quite remarkable." It's impossible to not re-read that a few times.

According to data,* the motherhood penalty amounts to about a 7% wage reduction per child. There is also some evidence of a fatherhood premium: a positive relationship between a man's wage and the number of children he has.

This happens because women are plagued by the gender norms that place men on the pedestal of capable, long-lasting and more involved employees than women who have to share their time at work between house and children. But is this fair? Is it right for women to price themselves less? Why are women taught that they are not as capable as men?

The discourse however is shifting and young women are choosing to assert themselves in relationships. Marriage, as an institution, is also up for some rethink. Women are seeking equal parenting. We will be addressing these issues as key roleplayers in the women's economy later in this book.

---

*https://www.oecd.org/newsroom/lackofsupportformotherhoodhurtingwomenscareerprospectsdespitegainsineducationandemploymentsaysoecd.htm

Men Are Sole Bread Earners: How It Is Not a Winning Situation

It is also important to note that the expectation from men to be the sole bread earner further drives their choice of high-paid jobs. In our society, men are ideally supposed to earn enough to provide for their family, and their wife's family. This pressure undermines a woman's ability and necessity to be financially independent. So, women tend to be satisfied in low-paying jobs themselves.

It is also wrong to think that the pressure on men to seek high paid jobs makes them a winner in every case. Studies have shown that the pressure to be responsible breadwinners impacts many men with mental health issues. Suicide rates among men who have the pressure to earn are 3.5% higher than women reeling under the pressure to fulfil the traditional roles.

Pankaj Kumar, an aspiring entrepreneur in Dehri-on-Sone, says that mental pressure is huge for him when it comes to marriage, family needs, and socialisation. "In society, men are judged in terms of their salary. Society will socialise with you if only you earn and earn well. I have sleepless nights thinking about my business and how I will earn enough to provide for my wife and family." He also says, "A man's happiness is totally dependent on the recession in the market. If there is a recession, earnings suffer a dip and men have to reel under the pressure of how they will be able to meet the increasing needs of the family."

"Marriage market too is obsessed with men who earn. It is almost time for me to get married. And I can't even imagine how difficult my life is going to be," he says.

Time to Change

So we need to understand that earning is not a gendered responsibility. It is okay for women to seek high-paid jobs too. Women need to unlearn the stereotypes and try to push their limits. If they surrender to the gender stereotypes, they will never be able to walk out of them successfully. Rather than assuming themselves to be less than men, if women start pushing their boundaries and competing with men, we will walk towards a future where men and women support the edifice of development equally.

Women's full and equal participation in all facets of society is a fundamental human right. Yet, around the world, from politics to entertainment to the workplace, women and girls are largely underrepresented.

Building a sustainable future for all means leaving no one behind. Women and girls are critical to finding solutions to the biggest challenges we face today and must be heard, valued, and celebrated throughout society to reflect their perspectives and choices for their future and that of the advancement of humanity.

chapter two

The Indian Marriage Fish Market

Middle-class India defines love as commitment to the man and his family for life. Love is the by-product of many social arrangements between families which is now popularly called the arranged-marriage culture. As a country, India has often been proud of the lowest divorce rates in the world but hardly allowed for a faceoff on how deeply unhappy and loveless some of these marriages are.

Most Indian women feel arranged marriages work because, after all, "parents know best". Well, it is true in some cases, but there are others who do fall in love and yet view getting married to their lovers as an impossible dream. The idea is inviting—you know the person, their habits, their preferences and also, not to forget, their sexual compatibility. If this is the case, then why do Indian women still opt for an arranged marriage fixed by their parents and "superiors"?

There are many reasons for it, including the overarching views of every family and extended family on who a girl should spend the rest of her life with. In the Netflix series *Indian Matchmaking*, matchmaker Sima Taparia reminds us again and again that marriage is a compromise. It's an adjustment, a rational decision, a thought-through settlement and that's why a family consent for the girl or groom is nearly a given.

She further adds how women must sit properly, smile nicely, talk softly, and create an aura of being likeable.

In India, marriages thrive on compromise. It puts the onus of success on the level of sacrifice, ability to negotiate and navigate, and doesn't hinge on love. It means "this doesn't match my expectations but I will settle somehow" instead of "this doesn't match my expectations but I am pleasantly surprised".

We are in the 2020s and yet some of the most viral conversations are happening about marriage-markets and bride-led stereotypes. Which essentially tells us that India, though by talking noisily about these issues might have taken some steps forward, but in its wider population this is only talk and no real on-the-ground changes have taken place.

In urban India, things have progressed a bit with new debates on how women want to claim their spaces and the rise of social and mass media conversations on the right for women to choose. Societies have shown signs of evolving. Freedom of choice is valued now more than before among the young. Some relatives or an aunty deciding who one should marry is a reality increasingly questioned and debunked by girls, though not always with 100% success.

It takes courage, but finally, women are asking

why a stranger should come over and evaluate how a girl fits into his life, whether or not she knows how to cook, if she will be modern and traditional at the same time. A bride in Maharashtra decided to cancel her wedding because the groom was drunk. A bride slapped the groom because he ridiculed her for "dancing" and another woman cancelled her arranged wedding because the groom's family didn't have bathrooms inside the house.

While these stories are few and far between, every now and then there are marriages that make it to the headlines for dowry death, bride burning, women being pushed to die by suicide, and many other horrific cases of domestic violence.

In India, the ideal setting of every arranged marriage has been—as reflected through countless Bollywood films—both sets of parents sitting in a drawing room, drinking tea and eating samosa (or sushi of late) and asking the to-be couple to step out to the garden (or a cafe) to "get to know each other".

"It's ridiculous," says Trisha Chatterjee, who just wrapped up her Masters in Political Science and is starting her PhD to avert the marriage offers. "We talk about this at home a lot but despite being a progressive family, when it comes to marriage, relatives and extended members weigh in. And so I am supposedly next on the marriage market."

"I get that a lot. If you are not doing anything with your life, may as well get married," Chatterjee says, as if marriage is like a vocational detour until one finds one's actual goal.

Chatterjee is not alone. Girls turn 20 and the

marriage conversation becomes the topic of every single holiday. A recent social media graphic that went viral stated, "They want to marry you off asap because they know as soon as you hit 25, you will realise you actually don't need a man."

How Arranged Marriages Promote Physical Stereotypes & Casteism

When a boy comes to see a girl, the first impressions are predominantly centred on body-shaming. Is the girl too fat, too thin, short, curly or long-haired, does she have fair skin or dark, and so on. Even in the 2020s, we as a country are far from beating "beauty" stereotypes deeply propagated by the shaadi market.

"At 5 feet 9 inches, my aunt's standard joke is how I will find a groom or will have to settle with a short guy and forever say goodbye to heels," shares Renu Singh who works in the social sector. "Each time a guy comes, my parents expect me to stay seated so I don't look so tall and of course do the standard deck-up drill like a doll, in front of unknown people."

Have we ever thought about men and women who are rejected for their facial features, skin colour, height, weight, curly hair, and other things? Colourism is a form of discrimination based on skin tone, perpetuated by the global beauty industry, where sales of skin-lightening products are projected to reach $8.9 billion by 2024.

In India, arranged marriages often lead to propagating colourism since brides are sought with a prescription. Most matrimonial ads talk of seeking a bride who's fair, pretty, and homely. A World Economic Forum article notes the existence of a wage gap linked to skin colour, which widens as the shade of the worker's skin darkens. This starts very early, because not only does society discriminate against women who are dark but the conditioning is so strong, that women internally break and start believing they are less worthy because of their skin colour.

"I am 23 and I was bullied in school because of my dark skin. I always felt worthless and thought I don't deserve anything good. I never talked with girls fearing that they will not like me. Worse, I always assumed I would not get a good-looking guy and was always willing to settle for less or was truly lucky if someone wanted to be with me."

Arranged Marriages Also Promote Casteism

Matrimonial ads are blatant about Marwaris preferring Marwaris, Sindhis prefering Sindhis, over others. "Looking for a tall Punjabi Sikh boy with a six-figure salary with no history of inter-caste relationships," went one advertisement. "Syrian Christian boy from Kottayam looking for a pretty, tall, fair Syrian Christian girl from Kerala. Girl should not want to work after children" was another. These are outright about their intent to marry within the community and about caste. It's not surprising that India has matrimonial websites focussed just on boys and girls from, for instance, the Brahmin caste or the Marwari community.

Years ago I met Mudrika, a young woman of 21, who was raised in a rich Hindu-Marwari family in

Chennai. At a time when people were new to flat-screen television, every single one of Mudrika's family rooms had one. They were eating food out of a can, while many middle-class Indians were still seeing it on the imported isle of an odd well-stocked supermarket and wondering when they would be able to afford foreign items. Mudrika had three sisters, and their father was a well-off Marwari businessman, with deep connections in the community.

Mudrika fell in love with a young boy who was neither rich nor Marwari. "It was not a match the family would approve of," shared Jesvita, her cousin, with me. "It came to this, that my father told Mudrika that she would have to make a choice between her family and this boy. This essentially meant, if she chose the guy, Mudrika would have no access to the money of the family. None at all." This was in the early 2000s. Mudrika and her sisters eventually married and fell in love with the boys their parents chose and have since "lived happily".

Who is to say whether the love marriage would have flopped, but instances like these are reminders of how our society functions. These stories are still steeped in the Indian fabric. As a result, many communities and families prefer to call marriage a social contract between families, villages, cities, and more than just a relationship between the couple.

There are many elements to caste in India and matrimony increasingly cements that. An essay*

---

*https://www.cambridge.org/core/journals/journal-of-asian-studies/article/abs/surplus-woman-female-sexuality-and-the-concept-of-endogamy/E1F0C997CF67690D3C1ADCFDE561908D published by Cambridge University Press talks of how upper castes in India used endogamy—the custom of marrying only within the limits of a local community, clan, or tribe—to preserve purity and "control female sexuality". Referencing BR Ambedkar, it notes that prohibition on intermarriage provided the basic framework for the development of the caste structure.

In an article,* sociologist Sharmila Rege, breaks downs what Ambedkar calls surplus women, those who are left after their husbands die. Ambedkar argues that exploitative institutions like sati and child marriage were introduced to "solve" this problem of the surplus woman.

As per Rege's essay, Ambedkar notes that the inferior status of women within caste groups produced two significant results. "Firstly, the surplus man and the surplus woman received differential treatment," or as Ambedkar puts it, 'man—as a maker of injunctions is most often above them all'. Secondly, because gendered violence became common and naturalised, castes were regarded as born not made, thus making them automatically exclusionary. By this, sati, and enforced and degraded widowhood became the chief means to disposing of surplus—practices that castes closest to Brahmins replicated variously, resulting in male superiority in all castes across the hierarchy. It is for this reason that Ambedkar saw caste's exclusionary violence and subjugation of women inherent in the very processes that lead to caste formation."

*https://scroll.in/article/902839/brahmanical-patriarchy-how-ambedkar-explained-the-links-between-caste-and-violence-against-women

When you are getting into an arranged marriage, there is a checklist. This includes that the girl should be known to the guy's family and what caste the couple is from. "For our families, caste was an important factor. It was also important for my family that the guy could look after me. I came from a privileged family and was looked after by my parents," said Rati Gupta. "Even girls who get attracted to a boy, first thing that comes to their mind is—will my parents approve this boy—what's his class, caste, and will that fit in ours."

A friend of mine, now 38, tells me of a horrific story about how deeply important caste is in our society. A well-educated Rajput family that used to travel around the world and were apparently intellectually progressive, shamed their daughter publicly. Their daughter married a Christian guy and her parents dumped all her belongings on the main road of the society and disowned her.

Why Do Young Girls Opt for Arranged Marriage?

"There is no such thing as a love marriage or an arranged marriage. It's just marriage and how two people make it work," says Yamini P Bhalerao, who is an author and works in a media house. "There is a sense of formality between a man and a wife. While we joke around, there's this line that you cannot cross. Somewhere there was this obligation—he is my husband, he is more mature, he knows better—that mindset comes through. It's also possible that it comes from not being financially empowered."

Yamini was brought up by two working parents

with careers, so why did she get into an arranged marriage? "When I was growing up, my parents were not too well off, like any middle-class parents. As a student I was mediocre. I opted for dental studies and my parents paid for it. They made it clear to me that they had no more money to pay for my higher studies. For my parents, who had two daughters, they would want to finish the cycle—raise me and get me married. I was not too ambitious. 'Dekhna shuru kar dete hai,' said my dad, and we started meeting people and I met this person who I genuinely liked. Since I didn't have many high aspirations and I didn't have another person in my life, I decided to marry.

"Many girls give in to marriage after college when they don't have a job waiting and their parents need to get this (marriage) done," says Yamini.

More recently, an even more interesting trend emerged. Many researchers have found that the youth today are increasingly opting for arranged marriages rather than love marriages. Some of this is attributed to young people not having enough time—while being focussed on their careers—to find a partner.

"I think we give very less credit to women," says Yamini. "They know their options laid out in front of them. Marriage is a practical decision. Marrying out of love is an impulsive decision that can be an uphill fight because a girl has to live up to that decision. Many of us had relationships in college knowing really well that this was going to last the duration of the course and then the couple would go their own way."

The modern Indian woman recognises that society has its ways and she is willing to adjust in order to thrive in that environment. "Survival is much more important than just marrying out of love," insists Yamini. There can be lifelong repercussions of taking a decision on love marriage/inter-caste marriage. Friends, parents, and families may stop talking to the girl because they eloped and married and permanently cut off ties.

As a result, women wonder if this love-relationship is worth it. There is so much working against women because of their gender, that they don't want more on their plate. Yamini says many women don't want to fight a battle they are going to lose. "If they go against society and home, is it really worth cutting off your life from one's world?"

Low Divorce Rates

Women are conditioned to acquiesce to all the decisions that their elders, especially men, take for them without raising any questions. Moreover, it is widely known that Indian parents are dominating and interfering and consider it their right to make decisions for their offspring. So it will not be wrong to say that arranged marriages in India are not about personal choice but about the choice that is fabricated by the consent of the family, community, caste, and religion—the ones who are not practically involved in the marital bond that is tied between two people.

India's divorce rate is at 1.1% and arranged marriages make for 90% of the marriages—two data points that have long been used to justify perpetuating the practice of arranged marriages.

If arranged marriages do not always involve the direct consent of the individuals being married, it cannot be said with complete guarantee that these marriages are happy and successful. The major reason behind this is its cause. In other words, the fact that an arranged marriage involves families and communities makes it difficult for a couple to choose divorce on an individual basis. And when it comes to women who already have less agency in terms of choosing the groom they marry, they end up living in marriages that are loveless, abusive, and unhappy. They are forced by their patriarchal conditioning, social, and familial pressure to adjust in a marriage which is considered to be the sole source of financial and social security for women. This can be further corroborated by the fact that in India, even though the divorce rates are low, the rate of domestic violence tops the crimes against women. According to NCRB data of 2019,* of the total 4.05 lakh cases of violence against women reported in India, 1.26 lakhs, which is equal to 30% of the total crimes perpetuated against women, were of domestic violence.

Not every arranged marriage is doomed and not every love marriage is one of dreams. But there are fundamental issues for every woman in every type of marriage which tie her down to society and familial expectations, driving home the idea of marriage as a compromise.

There is an absence of agency of women in arranged marriages. They are deprived of the right to speak

*https://ncrb.gov.in/sites/default/files/CII%202019%20Volume%201.pdf

against injustices such as domestic violence even though they are labeled as bahuranis or the keeper of the key to the tijori. Amidst this deprivation, it is important to consider the economic status of women in arranged marriages. Marriage in India is an important factor to decide whether a woman is financially empowered or not. According to a report by World Bank* released in June 2020, India's female labour force participation has decreased to 20.3%, which is the lowest in South Asia. Even though the enrollment of women in educational institutions has increased, their participation in the labour force has decreased. The major reasons behind this is that either women are not able to manage personal and professional life together or they are pressured by the families who disagree with the idea of women working after marriage.

It is believed that if a man's income is enough to take care of the family, there is no need for women to step out and earn. "How many times have I been told—your husband earns well, why do you need to work?" says Sunaina Dev, a young woman in the public relations industry. Once a woman is married, generally decisions for her life are taken by her husband and his family. So even if the woman wants to continue her job or pursue her education, the final call will be of the husband and the in-laws. Another survey of 2016** revealed that 20% of the families still agree with the idea that women should not work

*https://data.worldbank.org/indicator/sl.tlf.cact.fe.zs?locations=IN

**https://www.statista.com/statistics/733444/young-adults-attitudes-on-women-working-after-marriage-india/

after marriage while only 30% disagree. Taking care of the house, indulging in unpaid labour and taking care of the progeny are counted as the main duties and responsibilities of a woman while her job is sidelined as a hobby or secondary preference.

Another research by India Spend* notes that families do not prefer to get their women employed and frown upon those who choose to work outside. This shows the lack of support that women can expect from her parental family in her choice to continue her job. Even though women have legal rights on the parental and marital properties, they are never allowed the freedom to exercise it. This further pushes them back in their aim to be financially independent and be a decision-maker for themselves at least, if not for the family. So, in many arranged marriages—even as we see examples of change—which make the decisions and involvement of the family imperative, women do not have the agency to exercise their choice. Their voice is silenced by two fingers—one is that of gender inequality between her and the spouse, and the other is of social and familial pressure and lack of support. Hence, arranged marriages become a complex impediment in the financial empowerment of women.

The Dowry Factor

In India, when marriages happen without dowry, they make headlines. Nearly all weddings have sought an unsaid dowry exchange. While in-laws of the girl expect

*https://www.indiaspend.com/category/women-at-work

it, parents garb it in the concept of "gifts" to make their daughter's life "more comfortable".

On May 1, 1961, dowry was prohibited in India and the Dowry Prohibition Act was enacted that criminalised the practice of dowry. But more than six decades later, the dowry system and harassment that it breeds continues. Twenty women die every day as a result of harassment over dowry. They are either murdered or compelled to die by suicide.

The brutal reality of the dowry system is not the story of rural areas only. Even the educated family sitting in metropolitan cities like Delhi and Bangalore is harassing a woman for not bringing enough gold or money. There was a famous case that made it to the newspapers of a young air hostesses from a rich home in South Delhi who was forced to jump off a building as her husband wanted her money. Another young girl, from a wealthy family in Kolkata, died under mysterious circumstances after she refused to ask her own parents for more money for the boy's family. Closer home, I can hardly erase the memory of a young girl with two little children in my home town of Kapurthala in Punjab. Sabbo, in her late 20s, was burnt alive because she couldn't continue to fill the "tijori" of her in-laws by seeking money from her poor parents who were simple labourers. In a really disgusting case, a husband brought back other men to rape his wife because she couldn't give dowry.

One often wonders why dowry continues despite it being a criminal offence. Part of the answer lies in how dowry is packaged and passed in India.

Our society values traditions more than laws. Just

because dowry is an age-old practice, and nearly a given, many families refuse to let the law lead. Part of this tradition apparently came to exist because women were unemployed and couldn't fend for themselves. Dowry was to be paid as a price for the man to look after the woman. In today's world, it's become a business model. There are stories after stories about how women are "sold" to men who will take them to Canada if the parents give the groom's family a massive dowry. The boy's family in many cases are using this as a way to earn a livelihood and many cases have been reported of men remarrying again and again for dowry alone. In a Punjabi wedding, the banquet hall of a five-star hotel had a decked Mercedes car in the centre of the marriage party to show off how wealthy and "generous" the bride's family was. Turned out the groom and his family too had a role to play in drawing up this list of things.

From the day a girl is born, families start to hoard expensive dowries to show off their wealth and reputation in society. I remember my own mother buying French corning plates in sets of two for my sister and I. It's a different matter we never married in a set up where dowry was even a conversation. But my mom too was conditioned to "build" a "trousseau" because reputed families must send their daughters with enough for themselves.

There's also a bizarre but real factor of reputation. Size of dowry is linked not just with wealth but how reputed the families are. Perhaps wealth is the measure of reputation in this case.

There are still more excuses in the garb of which

dowry continues till today. I have personally witnessed how the pressure of dowry completely breaks women's families who cannot afford expensive things.

But today, women are slowly asking uncomfortable questions. Why should we follow a tradition that doesn't make sense in the present times? Haven't we already left behind many traditions related to clothes, food and lifestyle? Why not dowry? Does it not show that women's oppression prevails even today? Why can't families use the immense wealth they waste on dowries in educating their daughters?

There was a famous case in Indian Institute of Technology, Delhi, of a female PhD scholar who died by suicide due to dowry pressure from her husband's family. "We should have saved for her dowry not her PhD," said her father to the press with tears in his eyes.

Many women are forced to quit education so that money can be saved for their dowry. But the question that needs to be raised repeatedly is why is the dowry system prevalent even today? When it is already a criminal offence, why do families continue to objectify and suppress women in terms of gold? Even though parents believe that more dowry is equivalent to more happiness for their daughter, can a marriage based on amounts of gold ever be happy? Can a woman be happy in a family that demands dowry? Do we care about women's happiness and independence in the real sense of the term?

Pallavi Lahiri says when she and her husband got married, they couldn't afford a nanny since they had recently bought a new house. "The option was for me to stay at home and raise the child or for me to work and earn just enough to pay the babysitter. Since my career was still taking shape, I chose to stay at home."

Then she decided to change her field and take up a job full time. "I felt that things would have been different if I was in a different job that was well-paying, such as a job in a multinational. If I was paid a lot and could contribute more to the house, my position would have been different."

It is high time women stop compromising for the sake of their husbands and the family finances. It is high time we understand that dowry is a patriarchal practice that only oppresses women rather than ensuring their happiness. If you really want your daughters to be happy, then educate them, help them know about their legal rights and encourage them to raise their voice against anything that oppresses them. I am just another daughter whose family practises dowry. If I can oppose it, so can you.

Women often have to make difficult choices. And it is high time they start making them.

chapter three

Dear Parents, Stop Raising "Gharelu Daughters"

When I was growing up, even though my parents were very liberal and progressive, my mother made sure I could roll round chapattis (Indian bread) by the time I turned 15. She would often remind me about the importance of learning how to cook because "Log kya kahenge?" I can roll round chapattis with my eyes shut but why is that such a big asset? When I grew up and got married, I was fortunate to find a husband who cooked brilliantly and loved kitchens and knives, something that didn't interest me as much. This too became a point of contention because it was so difficult for my parents to see me enjoy my afternoon reading a book on the sofa with a gin and tonic while my husband drubbed up a mean biryani. This is the conditioning with which they were brought up and the same is what they were trained to pass on to their children. The man of the house has a role and the woman in the house has her own role and mixing or changing that equation leads to ripple effects. It's changing slowly but still comes down to an occasional celebration on social media or in cocktail gatherings.

Look at Puja's story. She lives in a thatched-roof house in Dehri-on-Sone in Bihar. Even before she learnt to hold a pencil, she knew how to clean utensils. She used to go with her mother to every house where her mother served as domestic help. As time passed, Pooja began to handle all her mother's work on her own. She along with one younger sister roamed from one house to another, to clean utensils, rooms, and eat some leftover food in return. Puja's father was a drunkard who earned nothing and sold off the ornaments at home at a low price to buy liquor for himself. And when he returned home all tipsy, he beat up Puja's mother. Brought up under such circumstances, Puja could never go to schools regularly. Even if she did, she had to quit because the burden of housework fell on her. Her mother and father rarely encouraged her to study, rather they pushed her into the labour sector from a very young age. Moreover, Puja's mother got her married at the age of 15 to an older but educated man. Even though the marital family promised to enrol Puja in a school, the promise remained unfulfilled even after years had passed.

Cunchan used to go to a government school in Dehri-on-Sone. But the reason behind it was to get the cycle that was being offered—in a government scheme—to girls free of cost. Her parents never inculcated the importance of education in her mind. So Cunchan could never focus on her education. She started working as domestic help at a young age and worked hard inside her home too. She had to do the work at different houses and then return to her home to feed her parents and brothers. Although she got married late, she is married to a man who is a drunkard and rarely earns a penny. The man even hits her after getting drunk which is why Cunchan returned to her maayka to escape from him and teach him a lesson. But her step went in vain when her own parents started forcing her to leave the maayka and adjust with her husband. She is caught between two sides, both equally toxic.

Arpita was brought up in a small family in Durgapur in West Bengal. Her family never encouraged her education and married her off at the age of 15. When the marriage was set, the man and his family pretended to be good. But after marriage Arpita was regularly harassed by her drunkard husband who used to sell her jewellery. At such a young age, Arpita had no understanding of what was happening with her. She also had a daughter so she was terrified to take any step. However, one day she did.

She walked out of her marital house with her daughter and started living with her mother. But her mother also after sometime started taunting her for staying at her parents' house after marriage. Somehow Arpita bore everything and educated herself through an online course. Today, she works in a parlour in Dehri-on-Sone and lives on her own with her daughter.

These stories are examples of how a lopsided upbringing can affect the lives of women forever. Parents in our society embody the role of leadership. They mentor kids, become their role models and the medium through which to understand the outside world. However, parents make wrong use of their power by being the ones who restrict the daughters. They misuse their authority by expecting their daughters to follow their demands and that of the society. Picture this: every Indian parent to the daughter—don't speak to strangers.

Daughters Raised as Burdens

Many Indian parents raise daughters as paraya dhan. They raise them as added burdens who have to go to some other family. Because of this, many parents are reluctant to invest in their daughters' education and employment. They value sons more since they are perceived to be the bhudape ka sahara. This is the reason why there is still a gender gap in the literacy rate of the country.

According to the 2011 Indian Census, the literacy figure in India was 74.04%. While the male literacy figure stood at 82.14%, the female literacy figure was a dismal 65.46%.

Moreover, daughters, hailing from the subservient gender, are expected to fulfil the norms set by tradition. They are expected to spend their time in learning how to be a good cook, good bahu, and good mother. Resilience, education, and employment is never seen as something that women must do. Parents as well as relatives and even political leaders expect daughters to be sanskari.

My friend and former colleague, Faye D'Souza, often reminds us on social media now that women should not be sushil, they must be stubborn.

Recently, the National Family Health Survey data revealed that the population of girls has become equal to that of men. This has happened for the first time. But is it really good news for us? If parents continue to subvert their daughters, their voices, and aims, then how can the increasing population of women lead to a better future? If girls continue to kill their dreams, choices, and ambitions, then how can we envision an equal society?

Education: A Distant Dream for Daughters

Even if some parents allow their daughters to be educated, the freedom is limited to the time when the girls attain a marriageable age. Many girls drop out of schools at an early age because of marriage, household responsibilities and financial difficulties at home. As per reports, girls drop out of school because, one, they are engaged in domestic activities (31.9%), two, they have financial constraints (18.4%), three, they are not interested in education (15.3%), and four, they get married (12.4%).

Last year, *SheThePeople* came across Radhika, a teacher at a government-aided school in Delhi who has been taking online classes for her students ever since schools closed due to lockdown. In the initial days of taking these classes, while she was still adjusting to the entire process, she came across a family of three daughters and one son that was reluctant to allow their daughters to take the lectures. They said that it was difficult to pay for the internet connection for four kids. And since girls have to ultimately marry into other families, their education is not important enough. As per reports, one crore women are at the verge of dropping out of school due to the pandemic.

If some parents educate their daughters, they do not let them pursue jobs. The reasons they give are that girls should not go out to work, earning is a man's job or that the future in-laws won't accept a working woman. In many Indian families, women are told that education is important but financial independence is not that necessary. It is always taken for granted that the husband's salary will be enough to provide for the wife's needs. The idea that the homemaker bahus are more gullible than the working ones is still prevalent in many Indian families. Besides, the working bahus are expected to shoulder household duties all on their own.

How Parents Are the Ones to Decide Whether a Daughter Will Work or Not

Now if some parents do allow their daughters to work, there are conditions in that too. They determine the kind of jobs they must pursue, the time they must go out and return and the kind of friends she should make. Many parents even say that working is allowed only until they are married. Once married, they must leave their jobs if in-laws expect them to. A woman is not even allowed to have a fall in her career because if the career of a woman doesn't work out in the first go, parents expect them to quit and get married.

Why do you have to do a job that won't give you the time to take care of your children and husband? This is what my mother said to me, annoyed at how my work keeps me too busy to do "enough" household chores. "Do a government job as it is easy, comfortable and women-friendly. It won't intervene in your life as a wife and mother." Now, I am used to these question and remarks, but why should a woman who wants to do something different even have to face such questions?

If a woman wants to be a lawyer, she is told that no man will agree to marry her. If she wants to be a journalist and travel back and forth to cover stories, she is reminded that her future in-laws won't approve of it and besides, who will take care of the children! "Aim for a 'simple' job," she is casually advised, "that doesn't require much effort and gives you time to take care of the house; after all a clean house is more important than your dreams." The idea of a Lakshman Rekha constricting a woman is so deeply rooted in the patriarchal society that any leap beyond it is always supervised and controlled. Today, if a woman is free enough to step out and gain an education, patriarchy controls her freedom not only by reminding her of her primary duties as a woman but also of her inferiority to men. Why is her duty as a wife or a mother considered as the primary aim of her life while education and career become secondary? Why should patriarchy decide which career is appropriate for a woman?

A "feminine job" is a legit term because patriarchy and sexism often denigrate women as incapable of a career in STEM, commerce, army, sports, and other fields that are traditionally masculine. They are thought to be suitable only for the comparatively "easier" streams like home science, arts, and others. It is because of these stereotypes that there are fewer women in STEM and fewer women aiming to build a career in arts and humanities as it is seen as "just a degree for the sake of education" after which they usually get married.

Harassment at workplaces or while out to work is one of the major reasons why families hesitate to allow their daughters to work. My mother's major reason behind not letting me pursue journalism was the reported cases of women journalists being threatened and abused while field reporting. But are women responsible for their own harassment and rape? Why should women be the ones to sacrifice their dreams because rapists cannot be punished?

How long will women sacrifice their dreams just because it is not feminine enough or their in-laws won't like it? Why can't we aim towards changing the patriarchal structures rather than learning to adjust to it?

Growing up as two sisters, as children in the armed forces, we had a very open upbringing. But raising your children in isolation from society doesn't help. Soon we would debate with our parents, and our families would advise them to "get the girls under control". I remember going to college and having the fear of being molested on India's many public buses. My dad bought me a bike and that let loose the whole extended family and friends to question my dad's "common sense" because apparently, he was "spoiling" his daughters by giving them "independence".

Marriage: A Major Milestone

For the longest time I have wondered why we celebrate marriage with so much investment and excitement when we don't do that for a girl's first job or her PhD. The major obstacle in women finding their calling is the necessity of marriage. Parents who are patriarchal expect their daughters to get married on time rather than investing in their education and career. They are expected to get married within their proverbial biological clock.

Marriage is seen as an answer to every problem in a woman's life. Be it mental health issues, financial problems or other issues. "When my husband and I were struggling to get our careers off, we were told, "Bacha paida karlo, sab theek ho jayega," says Karen Dmello, who has since moved out of Chennai and now lives abroad.

"Women are not raised to be independent but to be dependent on the man they marry. Even in childhood girls are expected to be dependent on male members of the family. Singlehood is rarely accepted as an option by parents," she adds.

The major reason behind parents' obsession with daughters' marriages is the idea that daughters are "someone else's property". Until and unless they are sent off to their "own" home, the woman is not settled in her life. This is problematic at so many levels—it's a gruesome reminder to a woman that her body is a present for someone else. That her existence isn't about her but someone else's happiness.

In the last few years there is a rise in the demand

for graduates who will also be *gharelu bahus*. How long will women sacrifice their dreams just because it is not feminine enough or their in-laws won't like it? Why can't we aim towards changing the patriarchal structures rather than learning to adjust to it?

As per data, the enrollment of girls in higher education has significantly increased from 39% to 46% from 2007 to 2014. More women are enrolling themselves for undergraduate courses. However, fewer women go for professional courses like Engineering, PhDs etc. According to a 2019 study,* around 42% of women were enrolled in PhDs.

Moreover, according to data by the World Bank, workforce participation of women has also dwindled from 30.27% in 1990 to 20.8% in 2019. It is also important to note here that even though parents enrol women in government-run colleges/schools, their attendance is lower than that of men as they consider education only as an asset to get them married. Most of these girls are forced to stay back to learn housework which is supposedly more important for her to get married into a good family.

So the only way change can be brought in is by educating the parents to change their mindset and raise girls as independent people and not as burdens. Parents need to break the shackles of patriarchy and look beyond it. They must know that there are many women who are using their education to change their

---

* https://timesofindia.indiatimes.com/home/education/news/gender-disparity-at-phd-level-men-dominate-by-a-huge-margin/articleshow/70535359.cms

world. Actor Ratna Pathak Shah rightly says, "Home is the nursery for patriarchy." And that's really where everything can be changed.

As soon as a woman crosses a certain age, marriage becomes an inevitable goal post in life. She is made to sit through various marriage meetings where a woman is judged based on her cooking skills, fairness, and beauty. And if a family rejects a woman, the rejection becomes a reason to shame and blame her. Families begin to question the woman's intentions, character and marriageability based on the judgements passed by a random family in a marriage meeting. This is something only parents can stand up against.

Why Shame Your Daughters?

Krutika Puri, 41, was bawling the morning I met her. She was done with her mother's taunts and couldn't believe that her own mom was the central reason for her to land up in this mess of emotions.

"You are way too ambitious, who will marry you? She would say things like, you wear short clothes and look like a slut," Krutika narrated. She is not alone and at first it's hard for many who don't have such an experience with their mother to imagine this. But 7 out 10 women complain about having issues with their mother over a difference of opinion on what to say, what to wear, and how to behave.

As parents give in to their eagerness to get their daughters married on time, they try to squeeze a woman's individuality to fit into the narrow patriarchal definition of a "good" woman even if this means that a woman has to lose her agency and freedom to choose.

The Change We Need

Like many things in life, marriage needs to be one of the many choices we make. Here's my personal story. At 21, I was married and divorced. It shook my household, my family, and to a great extent, left me wondering if I was that black sheep society constantly alluded to. My mother hid the divorce from every single person we knew. It was such a stigma.

Back in 2003, divorce was a horrific word and such cases were hidden under the carpet. My dad must have lost four kilos in two weeks worrying for me. But I was a woman who was determined to not let this "setback" in the eyes of society, define me. I worked, harder than ever, to prove I deserved every bit of my journalistic success. And I got there. I saw my parents move from deeply broken to confident of who I was becoming and how my identity had nothing to do with a man for many years after that break up.

There may be all kinds of data to suggest marriages by arrangement are truly the longest lasting or love marriages can be fickle but, at the end of the day, there is very little conversation to drive home the point—whatever the type of marriage, a woman should decide for herself.

It is high time that families start perceiving their daughters as individuals with agency. Parents need to understand that the definition of marriageability is wrong if it contorts a woman's freedom to be who she is. It is perhaps time we change how we determine a woman's marriageability. It should include a woman's choice, her freedom to be empowered and outspoken. None of these traits must be compromised when families define a woman's marriageability. Society needs to understand that a woman's happiness lies in her freedom and not in her confinement in a patriarchal marriage.

The Indian Human Development Survey in 2012 covered over 34,000 urban and rural women between the ages of 15 and 81, in 34 Indian states and union territories, with the aim of understanding marriage among other things. 73% of the women surveyed reported that their parents or relatives alone chose their husbands, while as few as 5% of women reported to have had sole control over choosing their husbands. 65% reported meeting their husband on the day of the wedding itself.

Family is always seen as a wholesome unit, nurturing love and support in all the members. It's our safe space and we tend to have a benevolent narrative of it. However, we often overlook the concept of family as a patriarchal and unequal institution that is oppressive to the women of the house. The power dynamics play a huge role here and mothers end up doing things no daughter likes to see them do. Women are conditioned to be submissive, soft, and docile, especially from the point in their life when they embrace motherhood. A mom is expected to not only be nurturing and caring, she must also be a role model for her children. Society tells men to see their moms as the definition of an "ideal woman" while girls are told to aspire to be like them some day.

Here are some things no daughter should have to see her mom do:

1. **Accepting Unjust Treatment in the Name of Adjustment:** Mothers often tell their daughters that when they marry, things will change and they will have to "adjust". The adjustment factor is somewhere so deeply rooted in their mindsets that they do not see it as problematic.
2. **Sacrificing Career for Family Rearing:** Mothers often depend on their husbands for financial support as in many Indian families women are discouraged from focussing on their career once they embrace motherhood. This dependent status is not seen as undesirable. The concept of motherhood is so romanticised that moms leave behind their careers and devote their lives to becoming the ideal mothers for their children.
3. **Asking for Permission:** On being asked if the kids can go out, you'll often find mothers replying, "I'll ask her father once." Moms often feel that they are powerless and have no agency, or lack confidence when it comes to making little or big decisions for the family. Even for basic things like going to the market or a friend's house etc., you'll find them asking for their husband's permission.
4. **Putting Themselves Last:** At children's birthday parties mothers will be found in the kitchen cooking while the fathers will be giggling with a glass of wine. Good food is offered to the fathers and leftovers are taken by the mothers. The whole notion of serving the family first and eating at the end is accepted by mothers and is sometimes even romanticised as "caretaking".

No girl likes to see her mother as an individual who hides her strength, lowers her voices, and censors her opinions, simply to make the opposite gender feel better about themselves. She has every right to live life on her own terms and encourage her daughter to do so as well.

chapter four

Measuring Housework

"Does the handle of a broom come printed with the words: 'To be operated by women only'?"

"What about the manual of the washing machine or gas stove? Then why is it that most men are not doing their share of the housework!"

Social worker Subarna Ghosh asked these questions in her Change.Org petition, urging India's Prime Minister to intervene and ask Indian men to share household chores. While Ghosh filed the petition during the early COVID-19 years, the questions she raises are universal, which is perhaps why 80,000 women signed it.

"The main issue was that there was a very clear disbalance in the division of labour at home. Clearly, I was mainly bearing the burden of housework. And it was not fair. I tried everything and nothing seemed to be working. There is this constant exhaustion at the end of the day and this feeling of being a part of a very unfair deal. That made me start the petition. I mean, housework is a very very valuable contribution to society and it is still being called a non-economic activity."*

No amount of money can make up for the drudgery of housework but we have finally begun a debate on why housework should be measured and if it is measured, what impact it can have on women. Could putting value to housework add to an ongoing power struggle between men and women? Will paid housework relegate women permanently as homemakers and further discourage them from having careers and aim for high-paying jobs? Economists have questioned the problems in accurately calculating the worth of a woman's unpaid work, raised the matter of how governments can afford such a programme and its sustainability as political parties in power change.

The everyday lives of women around the world share one important characteristic: unpaid care work is seen as a female responsibility. Around the world, women spend 2–10 times more** time on unpaid care work than men. This unequal distribution of caring responsibilities is linked to discriminatory social institutions and stereotypes based on gender roles.

One of the women who signed the petition said, "Women are working from home, managing the household chores, taking care of the children and all these things, besides following the commands of their

*https://www.bbc.com/news/world-asia-india-53469696 https://www.bbc.com/news/world-asia-india-53469696

**https://www.unwomen.org/en/news/in-focus/csw61/redistribute-unpaid-work

husbands. He would say, 'Get me coffee', 'Get me tea', 'Finish this', 'I want lunch by 1 o'clock', and she has to follow."*

Gender inequality in unpaid care work is the missing link in the analysis of gender gaps in labour outcomes, such as labour force participation, wages, and job quality. At the very core of it, it's all about changing cultures and mindsets. So tackling deeply entrenched gender norms and stereotypes is a first step in redistributing responsibilities for care and housework between women and men. But where are we on this entire journey?

Care work is the "hidden engine" that keeps the wheels of our economies, businesses, and societies turning. And it is driven by women and girls who, with little or no time to get an education, earn a decent living, be involved in their communities or have a say in how our societies are run, are trapped at the bottom of the economy.

Let's look at some numbers. According to an analysis by Oxfam,** women's unpaid labour is worth $10.9 trillion—three times the size of the global tech industry. According to the Organisation for Economic Cooperation and Development, an average woman spends 351.9 minutes, which is almost six hours, on unpaid labour per day, while a man spends only 52 minutes. In many cases, the time women spend per

*https://www.thequint.com/neon/gender/pm-modi-change-org-petition-to-tell-men-to-share-housework

**https://www.oxfam.org/en/not-all-gaps-are-created-equal-true-value-care-work

day on housework may even exceed what is legally allowed for the recognised workforce in India.*

American economist Joseph Stiglitz, who I have interviewed on many occasions, noted this with clarity back in 2007 when he said,** "Unpaid care work is both an important aspect of economic activity and an indispensable factor contributing to the well-being of individuals, their families and societies." Every single day people spend time cooking, cleaning, and caring for children, the ill, and the elderly. But unpaid care work is considered not relevant enough for policymaking, or is commonly left out of government agendas due to inability to count it by standard market work measures.

Could an assignment of payment acknowledge the opportunity costs of household work? In order to do housework or find a balance, women are generally forced to choose lower-paying options in the informal sector or just simply leave the workforce entirely. This is the kind of price women are paying to do housework because there isn't another choice. In many homes in India, the burden of house work is quick to come on young women, which also scuttles their ambitions and opportunities to learn and work because they must adhere to their house's needs.

What Are the Issues?

Krishna Ahooja Patel famously said this in the 1960s. "Women are half of the world's population, do two-

*https://www.shethepeople.tv/finance/paid-housework/

**https://www.oecd.org/Dev/Development-Gender/Unpaid_Care_Work.Pdf

thirds of the work, get one-tenth of the income, and are the owners of one percent of the property." Patel was a member of the Women's International League for Peace and Freedom and a lawyer who worked with the United Nations for over 25 years.

A lot of the issues women face when it comes to housework and its value stem from a highly conservative and bigoted system of sexual division labelled as "reproductive labour", where women are compelled to bear the undervalued, invisible and taken-for-granted weight of childcare, nurturing, and domestic chores, thereby easing men to devote themselves to "productive labour", a type of work that is recognised, dignified, paid, and appreciated way more.

Right from childhood, women are groomed to be good girls, housewives, good daughters, good mothers, and good partners where the definition of good—for most part—is based on compromise, leaning in, and being governed over.

Housework, therefore, becomes a great deal about power struggles—of how a man of the house demands a woman do her job. I simply cannot forget the story of a couple I stayed with for a short while. Protima, a mother to two, was a really prolific interior designer while her husband was in the armed forces. "Protima where are my shoes? Why have they not been polished?" yelled her husband one morning, throwing the entire house into an unruly din. Protima obediently brought his shoes for him. On a day it wasn't the shoes, it would be the salt in the food, the dirty clothes, or even just the children. The man always had a grouse about what was not right—in his perception—in the house.

"It's been 12 years and every single day it's been the same story," Protima confessed. "I wish I was not trained to believe that marriages and housework are my job, I might have been ejected out of this situation." After 15 years of this marriage, Protima filed for separation and built a career in interior designing at the age of 38, from scratch.

Not just subservience to their husbands, women are subjected to the likes and dislikes of the family members. Family structures force a woman to be the recipient of views and expectations of parents, in-laws, society, friends, "well-wishers" and many others. Keeping this in mind, many believe paying a minimum wage or salary for the services of homemakers might seem a good idea.

While Protima was a smart urban woman, somewhat aware of her ability to build a life of dignity by herself, not everyone is so empowered. 41-year-old Noorjahan from Mumbai was married off at 19 to a man who came home drunk every single day and beat her up. She has three children, all in their 20s and none work enough for a living. "I grew up in a well-off home and became poor the day I got married. Every single thing of mine was sold by my husband to drink. From having to not work to feed myself, I picked up the job of a nanny to make life happen." Earning changed her attitude towards life. "Money gave me power. Stepping outside of the house gave me agency I never had. Today I say no to anyone who forces me. But everyone doesn't get so lucky." While financial independence and what can lead to it, is another chapter in this book, what we do know is that paying for housework or the government valuing it can bring a basic level of dignity and respect to every woman in her relationship, and in her family.

Arguments for Valuing Housework

The demand for wages for housework was first raised in 1972, in a paper presented in the National Women's Liberation Conference in Manchester, by writer and activist Selma James. She also founded the International Wages for Housework Campaign, which continues to campaign for recognition and payment for all housework and care.

Selma James talks about why paying is better than any other situation in a video debate on housework. "Basic solution to the crisis of poverty and overwork was a wage for the work we were doing. We decided to discuss this in the women's movement. Mostly feminists thought it was a bad idea. That it would institutionalise us." She questions what could be worse than how women have been institutionalised by society in poverty and financial dependence.

I read this somewhere on social media and it struck a chord. Society started referring to moms as superheroes because it was easier to sit back and let us do everything while making it seem like a compliment rather than taking things off our plates or stepping up and helping us. Have women underserved themselves by believing in the superwoman culture? Have women been happy enough with credit, kudos, and thank yous from the world for cleaning, caring, and cooking in garb of love and family responsibilities? We women have a lot of trouble keeping our identity visible. We shy away from money. We shy away from asking our worth. One wonders if these have played into the manipulative hands of society.

There are, therefore, many good reasons to start thinking of putting financial value to a woman's work.

Prabha Kotiswaran, professor of Law and Social Justice at King's College London argues it's time for wages for the housework movement to be identified and that married women deserve a state-funded direct cash transfer. "These should not be in lieu of but in addition to other efforts to improve child care, and continued investments in workplace protection and other public infrastructure. This will help us open up the black box of marriage."

Kotiswaran links this to the many arguments also made in our chapter on Indian marriage systems where majority of Indian girls are faced with compulsory marriage by the time they hit the late 20s. There is the dowry factor and her life is pinned to the benevolence of her husband or his family. Kotiswaran, who received her undergraduate law degree in India from the National Law School University, argues that most Indian women have little or no financial support should they walk out of their marriages. A woman "will soon realise she has few economic rights. She has a limited right to maintenance access which is based on long waiting periods before courts for paltry amounts paid long after petitions have been filed with husbands hiding their assets. She will have no access to property bought by the couple to which she may have contributed with her unpaid work. When she goes back to her natal home, she will likely be resented. She is also likely to have lost her dowry and not be able to retrieve her streedhan."

Kotiswaran's context about rights and claims in India is important. She was speaking at a debate For and Against wages for housework. "In other parts of the world we can think of prenuptial agreements, employment and tax devices to account for unpaid work but it's unrealistic in a country where marriages are not registered or documented and work is mainly in the unorganised sector."

Her argument is for the government to pay the woman at the point of marriage rather than her having to look at her husband at the cusp of divorce for financial aid. She says such a cash transfer "will not be an obstacle to reforms and family law, to allow for a community property regime, where property acquired by either spouse during marriage should belong to both". She adds that this is because the baseline grant is nowhere near the replacement value of unpaid work. "These stark realities are not unknown to women in marriage. And most continue with marriage. I argue that during the marriage, grants can help improve the woman's economic bargaining power. The idea of monetising unpaid work will challenge the ideology of domesticity. It can help a woman set time boundaries for her unpaid work. It may help her learn skills or exit marriage."

This story of a young girl from Kolkata strengthens the arguments Kotiswaran makes. "My father beat up my mom very often and we had little or no choice because we didn't have money to live a life of dignity by ourselves," Mouni Sengupta, 21, shares in a Direct Message. "From the time I was 8 years old, I saw my father raise his hand on my mom but also bring his girlfriend to our house, with the full support of his entire family, with whom we unfortunately live. My mother is Marathi and my father is Bengali and their cultural differences, apart from economic differences, made it worse."

Sengupta and her mother still live in the same house. "We are in this because of the money. We don't have money, because my mother doesn't work. And I am not yet working as I am still in college. Years have passed, the domestic abuse has continued." Her mother does the entire housework and cooks for the large family and silently bears this torture. My DMs are full with such stories of suffering because women are forced to put up with husbands who run the house.

Arguments Against It?

Does valuing housework take away from the bigger responsibility of society and governments to create a level playing field of opportunities for women? Does it relegate women to beings who should do housework because suddenly there may be a remuneration for it?

As I write this chapter, I am staring at a pile of dishes waiting to be washed. Someone has got to do it. While in homes like mine there is external paid help and we as a couple contribute our own share of work, it's certainly not the case with most Indian homes. Paying women wages for doing housework presumes that women are and should be the ones who do the housework, and that they do not already have a paying job. That too can be problematic.

In most families in India today, men and women are not sharing housework and many women may want to work outside the home but simply cannot because the housework is way too much.

Saumya Kapoor Mehta, the head of the Initiative for What Works to Advance Women and Girls in the Economy agrees that there should be a value associated with work rather than the role a woman is performing. A notional wage makes the idea empowering, she says.

But Mehta raises some important issues when it comes to the repercussions of valuing housework. "State will absolve itself of the responsibility of offering opportunities in the labour market that are suitable for women, thereby reducing the wide expanse of roles women can come to play with equal if not better talent." This will also put a question mark on the movement of seeking equal wages.

How does one assign a notional value? While raising a question on the methodology, Mehta raises some economic aspects. "Do I assign an imputed cost this woman is spending in raising her children, or in fetching water or firewood? In which case how do I break down the smaller processes of labour? It's not just going and fetching water, I might have to plan it through, not just the travel time, what vessel to get. There are laborious processes linked to it."

How does one value the opportunity or cost of time depending on what the woman wants to do? Does she want to do something like a leisure activity? And is the opportunity cost to be calculated on that basis?

Milad Doroudian, a writer, columnist and historian, who also writes in *The New York Times,* raises some of the more emotional questions which have trickled into this debate. "If monetary value were placed on housework, marriage would be an employee-employer relationship, creating disparity and inequality since money means power." He adds, "Children would feel dejected when they learn that the person who loves them, and whom they have called mother or father, was in fact getting paid to raise them."

Journalist Porche Moran argues that it is a complicated proposal that requires examination. "For starters, every homemaker has different responsibilities depending on their family's circumstances. How would the government determine a monetary value for housework that would fit every family?"

Where Has this Taken Place?

A diverse group, which made up the Global Women's Strike in Venezuela, including women from India among other countries, led a feminist revolution to force Hugo Chavez to grant* housewives social security. Under this inclusion in the Constitution of the Bolivarian Republic of Venezuela, the State guarantees equality and equity between men and women in the exercise of their right to work. "The State recognizes work in the home as an economic activity that creates added values and produces social welfare and wealth. Housewives are entitled to Social Security."

*http://www.globalwomenstrike.net/

One approach is the provision of welfare payments or transfers to enable families to care for vulnerable groups, exemplified by Kenya's Cash Transfer for Orphans and Vulnerable Children. A few other social security programmes in Nepal provide benefits for particular categories of women, such as the elderly allowance, with affirmative provision for women over 60 who are widows; the single women allowance for women over 40 who have never been married or are separated; and the disability allowance. None of these programmes, however, explicitly recognise women's role in caring, perhaps because measurement remains an issue? Some of these programs are struggling with more fundamental queries of providing allowances without catering to meaningful on-the-ground job opportunities, child care, and also access to clean and hygienic bathrooms at work.

More Care Work, Less Career?

"When my husband and I were starting out our careers, I got pregnant," says Vaishali Bhardwaj who trained in human resource management. "Somehow the question was never about *if* I wanted to work. It was about who was earning more and therefore the more important job. I lost that battle." Bhardwaj and her husband didn't explore a baby-help because the family elders believed children "needed mothers and not nannies to look after". With another child on the way, Bhardwaj had no career for over 10 years after her marriage.

Gender inequalities in unpaid care work are also

linked to gender gaps in labour force participation. The higher the inequality in distribution of care responsibilities between women and men, the higher the gender gaps in labour force participation. The OECD report notes that in countries where women spend almost eight times the amount of time on unpaid care activities than men, they represent only 35% of the active working population.

"The unequal distribution of caring responsibilities also provides an important clue to understanding why reduced gender gaps in education have not led to reduced gender gaps in employment in certain countries. Women in countries with high responsibility for unpaid care work are more likely to have lower levels of economic activity. So despite decreasing the gender gap in education, these countries have not been able to maximise the returns from this investment and have persistent gender gaps in employment outcomes."

"I gave up my job because my ailing mother needed full time support," says Gauri Singhal who is a journalist in Pune. Singhal literally got wiped out of the organised workforce she was part of. Even among the wealthier and more educated households, inequalities in caring responsibilities persist: women contribute more than 60% of the time devoted to housework and care, irrespective of their employment status, income, or education levels.

Housework is not only about cooking and cleaning but also about maintaining the house, managing the budget and saving money. Housework and care work supports the economy of the family too and hence of the nation too.

As per the OECD report, in countries where women spend twice as much time as men in caring activities, they earn only 65% of what their male counterparts earn for the same job. This drops to 40% when women are spending five times the amount of time on unpaid care work (for full-time employees).

Households, Biases and Progressive Possibilities

Biases come to play in this very quickly. India's son bias discriminates against girls who are raised to believe their job is to do the housework. "I have been conditioned to get up and serve water to the guests when they are home," entrepreneur and UN activist Navya Naveli Nanda says about how deep-rooted girl stereotypes are. "My brother will be around but no one will ask him." Naveli belongs to one of India's most prestigious film families, the Bachchans. Her story and that of Ridhima from a village outside of Jaipur is no different.

Women, by default, are expected to be in charge of household work, even when they have work-schedules that are hectic and sometimes even busier than those of their male counterparts.

Take the example of our family WhatsApp groups. There's always that young guy who is glorified for the one time he made breakfast or made the bed. There's many examples of that kind. What's so comic about a full-grown adult man of the 21st century being clueless about purchasing vegetables or not knowing one bean from the other?

It can be argued in their defence that these men

and boys have probably spent their entire lives enjoying the benefits of a patriarchal system that allows them to keep their lives perfectly intact, without having to know any of the essentials of housework.

We need to stop making fun of men who are taught life-skills and share or contribute to housework. Indian society mocks a man who prefers to cook or clean and is understanding of his wife's time, as "joru ka ghulam" i.e., a man who is subservient to his wife. In joint family gossip one has heard this time and again that a man who agrees with the challenges of his wife is "henpecked". These are all testimony to the lop-sidedness of a systemic cycle of patriarchy that feeds on creating more and more biases.

Can Populist Politics Play a Part?

Paying for housework is also a populist promise now. Pandering to a female vote has become a high priority for leaders who have started including many women-centric issues in their manifestos. One of India's super star actors-turned-politician, Kamal Haasan, has triggered a national debate on paying or not for housework by bringing it into his manifesto.

His punt? Any efforts to value housework—notwithstanding an intellectual debate on its merits and demerits—will most certainly be approved by the female electorate.

The country's democracy is seeing a change in voting patterns and women are coming out to express their ballot in big numbers. In India, the number of women voters increased from 47% to 48.13% as per statistics out in 2019. More women are voting* than before, and one hopes this increase in political capital could mean that their rights and issues are no longer an afterthought for policymakers.

India's prime ministerial elections in the past have seen an increase in women voters. Many significant states are clocking a change, including those like Bihar, Rajasthan, Odisha, and Tamil Nadu. In Assam, Himanta Biswa Sarma (chief minister of Assam at time of publication of this book) announced his victory credit to women voters.

Sarma said, "I was confident that women will vote for us heavily, irrespective of their caste, creed, and religion. Women as a class have voted in favour of the BJP in this election because of our government's policies of empowerment."

In West Bengal as well, many have credited high women turnout for the victory of Mamata Banerjee-led Trinamool Congress (TMC). Bengal voted for Bengal's own daughter; one of the TMC campaign pitches was "Bangla Nijer Meyekei Chay" or Bengal wants her own daughter. Bangla or Bengal is the motherland and the State—in sync with the party's motto "Ma, Mati, Manush" or "Mother, Motherland, People"—that voted for her daughter, who is otherwise the synonymous Didi or elder sister, pitted against the BJP "bhumiputras" or the sons of the soil.

In Tamil Nadu, female voters were offered free and subsidised transport for women; free home appliances,

* https://indianexpress.com/article/opinion/the-rise-of-the-female-voting-bloc-elections-7309796/

increase in maternity benefits, and reservation for women in government jobs were some of the other electoral promises made in a bid to win women's votes.

These examples are illustrative of how women have become a remarkable bloc that politicians now want to squarely address. Paying for housework is an area they have their eyes on. One may add that politicians are using this as a poll vault but are very unsure on how to deliver these promises other than in the form of freebies and house appliances.

How Can We Change This?

Society is on the move and people are recognising why it pays to share work. The process is slow but the conversation has well begun. I know of stories where women refuse marriage in villages if the groom's family doesn't have an ensuite toilet. Girls are refusing to marry in homes where wifi is restricted or where the boy doesn't give her the option to work.

Care should not be considered only as a burden and this central activity for well-being should be redistributed between men and women.

Government must create awareness about a scheme targeted to making housework valuable for the woman who chooses to stay at home. Nivruti Naik lives in Mumbai along with her husband and currently looks after their three children. Having finished her Masters in Arts, she got married and since then has never worked. Rising prices of everyday essentials has families scrambling for more. "Any leader who promises any funds for housework, we will be out there to support and take any cash transfers that help our monthly budgets."

A researcher writes in *Manorama*, that to address this exploitation, demand for remuneration for housework was strategically employed to serve three purposes* the first of which included efforts to make domestic and unpaid care work visible and enhance the dignity of women. Two, to enable fair redistribution of wealth and reduce women's economic dependency, leading to greater autonomy. And three, to bring about a change in power relations and pave the way towards women's refusal to do housework itself.

Better access to public services, child care and care for the elder is one approach. Longer school days or expanded pre-school hours are alternatives for public day-care. Equal amounts of maternity and paternity leave increase women's employment by increasing employer incentives to hire women. In Sweden, for example, a minimum share of available parental leave is reserved for fathers on a "use it or lose it" basis, encouraging an equal sharing of caring responsibilities. Family-friendly working conditions enable parents to balance their working hours and caring responsibilities

The women and men who devote their days to keeping their households in order deserve respect and appreciation.

---

*https://www.manoramayearbook.in/india/special-articles/2021/01/20/salary-for-homemakers-analysis.html

chapter five

Curse of the Saasu Ma

The Mother-In-Law Factor

Actor Sameera Reddy took a five year break to raise her children after marriage. She made a choice. She needn't have got off work since she had a supporting husband, an understanding mother-in-law (MIL), and a larger extended family to help raise her children when she would get busy or wanted to take a break. But not all women are like Sameera. Most married women have no choice. They have families that leave them by themselves to work, to do housework, cook for the family, to raise children, and have careers, if at all. Interestingly, the woman's freedom to step out, work, meet other people and even access to healthcare could be deeply connected with how her mother-in-law is. It's this relationship that has come to epitomise the success of a woman after her marriage.

I read something that compressed this issue into a simple Instagram post.

"The girl is so educated, she won't make a good daughter-in-law."

Translated: Since she is educated she must be aware of her rights and won't accept slavery under the garb of marriage.

The saas-bahu relationship in Indian society is the stuff legends and daily soaps are made of. A lot is said about this love-hate relationship, and the narrative for most of history is stereotypical. The iron-fisted mother-in-law finds her son's wife an intrusion into her own ways of working and that's the starting point of a dysfunctional relationship where the saasu ma wants to unleash her own repressed anger and give the daughter-in-law a taste of what she got as a young bride from her own mother-in-law. This is a blueprint for many households. We accept this relationship being contentious at face value, simply because we are conditioned to see it that way.

Never do we stop to think about why this relationship is depicted in such a way, nor the effects it has on day-to-day life. The trope of the so-called "monster-in-law" is so commonplace that the effects of a mother-in-law who isn't that, are transformational.

World Bank professor, S Anukriti, led a paper that reveals how mothers-in-law in India have a big say in who a daughter-in-law interacts with and whether or not she should go to a healthcare facility all by herself. The paper is based on a study of 671 participants from Uttar Pradesh's Jaunpur and spotlights the challenges faced by women in the hinterland in forming social connections that can help them through issues like fertility and family planning.

The study shows that mummy ji's expectations of their daughters-in-law (DIL), how many children she should have and what behaviour she must display, are big factors in a woman's life. In fact, the mother-in-law may have more influence on a woman than even her husband in many arranged marriages. The rate of arranged marriages in India is nearly 90% as per one survey.*

When a woman is married into her new home, she is often told that she isn't just marrying a man but a family, and at times, a village (figuratively speaking). It's made amply clear to the woman that she will have to look after the kitchen and household.

Here's the story of Madhu (name changed) who grew up in Kolkata. Her father worked in an engineering company while her mom was a housewife. Madhu and I got to know each other through a friend at a time when Madhu was working with an airline company. She was dating a boy who was too scared to ask her to marry him because his parents simply wanted a woman to "handle" the house while they ran their doctor's clinic. This was a big dilemma for a young independent Madhu who was raised to have a career and be financially independent. The options

---

*https://medium.com/@solutionswebomania/current-trends-arranged-marriages-in-india-e0435d455e8e%23:~:text=Arranged%2520Marriage%2520Statistics:&text=55%2525%2520of%2520the%2520marriages%2520that,world%2520today%2520 are %2520arranged%2520marriages.&text=The%2520rate%2520of%2520arranged%2520marriages%2520in%2520India%2520is%252090%2525.&text= In%2520an%2520arranged%2520marriage,%2520the,woman%2520in%2520the%2520 formed%2520relationship.

ahead of her? Leave the man she loves or start living on his parents' terms. Like in many households in India, boys are raised to follow their parents and in matters of marriage, not speak up against them. This young man took six months of conversations to finally muster courage and speak to his mother about his relationship with Madhu.

The boy's parents asked the girl's parents for all sorts of things—from certificates of fixed deposits as proof of "financial security" to seeking the girl's consent to "take charge of the house". After many unpleasant situations, the couple moved out to live independently. "I was driven out. I learnt to multi-task and struggle with my job, my two daughters, and other commitments of life," says Madhu. "My working mother-in-law couldn't recognise why a career was important for me," she adds ironically. "Had things been better she and I would have lived under the same roof, created an external support system and had our own careers."

On social media, a woman named Mahima puts the crux of this issue as conditioning. "You will always have guilt tied to every decision you make for your own betterment cause we are raised to be obedient daughters, trained to be compliant wives, and our value is determined by how well we follow instructions."

A lot of the times the issues between mother-in-law and daughter-in-law are purely based on ego clashes. For some, it's who will "bow" down, who will follow whose instructions, while for others, it's about the control over the son or husband. The conflict often emerges from an expectation that each is criticising or undermining the other, but this mutual unease may have less to do with actual attitudes and far more to do with persistent female norms that few of us manage to shake off completely.

Sameera Reddy's relationship with her mother-in-law, Manjri Varde, wasn't a hit on day one. But as she says, we learnt about each other and became tolerant about who we both were. In Indian households it's a power game between DIL and MIL.

Part of the power equation was diffused because Varde was independent herself and ran a business alongside being a celebrated artist. "I have been single and independent for a long time and so there was no power game in ours," says Varde, an artist who exhibits in Mumbai.

But did they have to draw boundaries? How did they do that?

"Giving space is very important," Varde says. "It also stems from the saasu and the daughter-in-law having a power struggle about the son. I had my own house. I was financially okay. Even though we all live together, the house is mine, it's in my own name. If there is that financial security, then in which case, I knew I had my own house, I don't have to go anywhere. I was financially independent. You know when you have children, you know they will grow up. So it was important for me to be financially independent. And that made me secure in my position."

As Varde adds, setting boundaries doesn't happen overnight, since it's not just about drawing lines. It takes confidence, conditioning and conversations over years and decades. "We have been setting boundaries through generations. My mom was independent. Every decision for me therefore was one of clarity and fearlessness whether it was the job, or the money in your account etc."

Manjri talks about "a sense of belonging and trust at a foundation level. You are living in the same house, we have to respect each other." She adds, "In the practical matter of things this is important. You don't have to touch my feet but if you make sure on the table there is food that I like and you don't like, then that makes a big difference and reflects where you are coming from." In that spirit, Varde says, the intent is visible on both ends to make this work.

Sameera is the mother of two small children and she admits, becoming a mom and entering a new household, all can be overwhelming for any woman. "We are not perfect, we have taken a while to get to this point and it comes with communication. It's taken us a bit of back and forth, stepping back and stepping forward."

"Simply because your spouse has a parent does not mean they need to be involved in your every move," says Nimrit Jalan, 31, who lives in a joint family in Udaipur. She takes the practical road in relationships. "Learn to communicate what needs to be communicated, and establish the kind of relationship that suits your emotional and physical needs. In these situations, you have to learn to lead, not to be led."

Jalan shares how in-laws interfere more when you don't draw the line. "A lot of mothers-in-law are curious when you are going to have babies. They even want to know when you're 'trying' a.k.a. having sex. I mean, why is this even their concern?"

What Does Research Tell Us?

That in-law tensions hit women hardest. Dr Terri Apter, a psychologist and senior tutor at Cambridge University, researched hundreds of families which showed that two-thirds of daughters-in-law believed that their husband's mother frequently exhibited jealous, maternal love towards their sons.

But why is the most difficult in-law tension between mother-in-law and daughter-in-law? Part of the conflict has its roots in the mother/son relationship, which contains an element of romance in a way that a mother and daughter bond does not, said Apter in an interview to *The Guardian*.* "This unique dynamic can trigger competition when another woman becomes the new closest kin," says the author of a book called *What Do You Want from Me?*

What's the Role of the Son?

The MIL-DIL relationship is so negatively portrayed that the son is absolved from any responsibility. 31-year-old Nalini, who lives in a Delhi suburb in a joint family says, "I have nothing against my in-laws and accept the fact that we have different points of view because of generation-gap. But I am really upset by the way my husband handles the arguments between my mother-in-law and I. It is an unspoken rule that he would only take her side and later console me in the bedroom. Recently, she spoke something against

*https://www.theguardian.com/lifeandstyle/2008/nov/30/women-family

my parents and my husband expected me to stay quiet and kept mum himself. I felt very disgusted and it is obviously ruining my married life."

While Nalini's experience is about her personal relationship with her husband, the responsibility of children adds to the pressures on a woman in a big way too. Parenthood is undoubtedly a colossal responsibility for a couple but every time a child makes a mistake, we blame the mother.

Raising a child is a mammoth task for both the mother and father. Hence, when kids achieve something, bring laurels or get praised, the parents are elated and proud. In fact, they consider it their own accomplishment. Not just the parents themselves, but the society also applauds the parents. However, when the child does something wrong, most of the times, the mother gets the blame.

A common occurrence in Indian households is that when a child does anything that is worthy of praise, a father would usually say something on the lines of, "Mere beti/bete ne kamaal kar diya!" ("My daughter/son has done a great job!") or "Mujhe mere beti/bete par naaz hain." ("I am proud of my daughter/son.") Evidently, the father takes pride in his child's achievement. Although he might also include the mother in the verbal expression of his parental self-credit by saying "hum/humaare" (our) instead of "main/mera" (my/mine), he would still associate himself with the feat.

On the other hand, when a child does something wrong, the father would say something to the mother like, "Dekho kya kiya hain tumhare beti/bete ne!" ("Look what your daughter/son has done!") or "Apne beti/bete ko kuch sikhao! Tumhara bachcha haat se phisal raha hain!" ("Teach your daughter/son. She/he is getting out of control!")

In fact, other family members, especially the mother-in-law, also tend to blame and rebuke the mother of the child. This way, fathers not only absolve themselves from the accountability for what goes wrong, but also conveniently put the entire blame on the mother, as though it's her fault that the child did something wrong.

Piya Vaidyanathan, 27, is a banker based out of Bangalore who recently got married. She says not only does she have significant responsibility in her married home but also as a daughter the overall pressure on her has gone up. "Our families have significant expectations of their adult children. So much rests on daughters, especially to be caregivers. Families also expect us to provide manual labour and to visit constantly—regardless of our physical abilities, stress status, children, and job."

"Our lives change the day we get married and from having a three-member family, we suddenly go to having ten people who we are somehow responsible for, just how is that fair to a girl?" Vaidyanathan asks.

Most women we spoke to said a lot of this can be bypassed if the MIL is supportive of her DIL's needs and helps create a positive system around her life in her new home.

Does the Father-in-Law Have a Role?

It's not a subject that's seen much research but anecdotally there are examples of fathers-in-law interfering with the economic ambitions of daughters-in-law. One woman, Anita (name changed on request), who works in the PR business, shares that when a woman doesn't have a voice, it's the MIL who intimidates her but if a woman does have a voice, it's the father-in-law who plays hell into her life.

"My relationship with my mother-in-law has improved over the years. It started on a rough patch as I was not the domesticated daughter-in-law she expected, coupled with her insecurity issues about sharing her son and only child with me. It was a difficult time mentally, and it took a toll on my work while working in a prestigious MNC. But things started to change once I became pregnant, and she was overjoyed with my daughter's birth. She'd always craved a girl child," Anita shares, who then moved to the United States of America with her husband and daughter, an experience she says completely changed the person she was.

"The US is an individualistic society, and I've learned to become like that and assertive as well. By the time we returned and lived with my in-laws, it was now my father-in-law who felt threatened with my new independent and assertive persona.

"He did try to intimidate me and abuse my family and me, and I didn't take it lying down. I complained to my husband and maintained a distance from my father-in-law. I was now dealing with an insecure and jealous father-in-law, who seemed fine when I was more demure at the beginning of my marriage. My mother-in-law and I are a working team at home now. I don't deal with them directly and let my husband handle his parents."

Here's how it all played into Anita's career indirectly. Its psychological impact, its strain on familial relationships, especially on her FIL and her husband's.

"As far as my career is concerned, I don't get any support from my in-laws, but my husband is supportive. Living in the US has taught me to be independent, and I live in a joint family like how I lived back in the States. I'm not dependent on my in-laws, and if I need to confide in anyone, I have my husband, who I can trust. I don't overextend myself and don't go out of my way for anyone at the risk of my wellbeing and career. I'm still pursuing my writing dreams while maintaining a full-time job and taking care of the home. But first, you need to take a stand for yourself and set the boundaries. It's essential to have a spouse who's supportive of you and your choices."

All About the Money?

Going back to Sameera Reddy, who makes an interesting observation about how in-laws control their daughters-in law. "The control comes from the money in Indian society. Bahu is controlled by that money, with the gold. You will get our jewellery sets only if you do this. You be subservient because this is what you will get in return. This needs to change."

Women most often are the ones who adjust their schedules and make compromises when the needs of children and other family members collide with work, according to data from the Pew Research Center.

Mothers Face More Career Disruptions than Fathers

A big factor is the way that society views the bond between mothers and their children. In 2012, Pew ran a survey in America where the majority (79%) rejected the notion* that women should return to their traditional role in society, that is, childbearing and household activities. Yet when they were asked what is best for young children, very few adults (16%) said that having a mother who works full-time is the "ideal situation". Some 42% said that having a mother who works part-time is ideal and 33% said what's best for young children is to have a mother who doesn't work at all. Even among full-time working moms, only about one-in-five (22%) said that having a full-time working mother is ideal for young children.

Now this is no different than in the story scripted in India. "When I got married, it was made amply clear to me, that after children are born I would have to quit my job and look after them," says 31-year-old Radhika Panjabi based in Chandigarh. "It's not even up for debate. No one was interested in speaking to me, mellowing the blow or having a conversation about other possibilities."

"My mother didn't miss a single opportunity to tell me that she was grooming me to marry and every time I retaliated, she would say 'Your mother-in-law will set you right. You will realise the importance of your

*https://www.pewresearch.org/politics/2012/06/04/section-1-understanding-the-partisan-divide-over-american-values/

mother when you meet a terror of a mother-in-law.'" That is Priyanka Dhar, 21, who doesn't want to marry or even have a partner because she doesn't believe the trope she is fed will be or can be any different.

Thirty-year-old Dhristi Pathak's (name changed on request) mother-in-law had problems with her office timings. Hers was an arranged marriage and soon after, she was taunted for late working hours and even more if she had to stay back for an office get-together. "One day, my in-laws ordered me to leave my job, because they felt that it wasn't good for a woman to come home late," says Pathak. "The girl should return before her husband and you must also do some household chores." Not only did this rock Pathak's relationship with her in-laws, it created distrust between her and her husband.

Today, when there are no kingdoms at war and women are much more than patriarchy's subordinates, it makes no sense to glorify a son-in-law while demeaning the daughters. But the start of this conversation happens with our own mothers.

What does it take for society to belittle the daughters in the families? A son, a jamai raja, and the mindset that works on the ideologies of male-child preference. No matter how talented, successful and happy on her own a woman is, desi parents leave no stone unturned to belittle her in comparison with her male counterparts. If a male child isn't enough to deprive a daughter of her rights in a family and society, jamai rajas become the new patriarchs who are always glorified and prioritised over daughters.

Desi moms police their daughters for almost

everything that they do while glorifying sons-in-law for just being a man who married and rescued their naive daughters.

Many of us have personally witnessed how families normalise the dominance of a son-in-law in a daughter's family, so much that he is never questioned for the evident mistakes that he commits. A son-in-law in my family is welcomed and served as a prince if he resides at his in-laws' home even for a day and often unwillingly. All his choices and priorities are kept in mind and the entire family works together to ensure that he doesn't feel any kind of discomfort. The daughter is expected to serve him first rather than spending time with her parents or lying down in her own room if unwell.

Not All Mothers-in-Law

In the early 2 CE, the Roman poet Juvenal wrote, "Give up all hope of peace so long as your mother-in-law is alive."* Clearly, the stereotyping began long ago in history, but it needn't have. Because? Not all mothers-in-laws are out there to make life hell for women. I for one, have had two mothers-in-law from two separate marriages and both did not fit the negative stereotypes.

No, none were demigods but both were sharp, practical, and content women who had identities of their own—one was a voracious reader and teacher, while the other was a writer and publisher. While it's true there are many mothers-in-law and daughters-in-

*https://sourcebooks.fordham.edu/ancient/juvenal-satvi..asp

law who don't get along, there are many who do, past some plainspeak and boundaries.

Women in India are expected to adapt to their matrimonial household unconditionally. Seldom do people, even women themselves, talk about how unreasonable this pressure is to adjust according to a culture and lifestyle that you are not used to.

My in-laws recognised this and made an extra effort to understand my point of view. One other thing that I did was to be myself and not pretend to be someone's bahu or someone who was an "ideal" person. I was totally in with my flaws, my real self and that really helped our individual adjustments to each other.

Yamini Pustake Bhalerao, 38, a full-time writer, moved in with her in-laws and her new baby because she had no childcare. "Only when my in-laws moved in with us and my mother-in-law began shouldering household and childcare duties alongside me, was I able to take up a job."

She adds, "A lot of working women will nod in approval when I say that modern mother-in-law and daughter-in-law relationship goes beyond the saas-bahu saga that we have grown up watching on television, where one party is projected as a predator and other as a victim. Pop culture has played a big role in twisting the narrative here."

Pranoti Gill (name changed on request), 33, who lives in Jalandhar, shares how levels of family discrimination double when caste gets involved. Gill reinforces the notion Dalit feminist Jyoti Lanjewar has previously articulated, that "Dalit women are also Dalits in relation to Dalit men within the Dalit community."

On the one hand, there are stories of struggles of mothering that Gill grew up with, drawing inspiration from, to become stronger. A Dalit woman, while narrating the past,* tries to negotiate a direction for the future, and her mother's story is the pedestal on which her life story depends.

"The struggle of the mother is an integral part of a marginalised woman's life but then you get married and your mother-in-law makes your existence about caste."

"In Indian society, girls are told they are 'leaving' their own home and once 'they arrive' at their in-laws, they would need to 'adjust' to their taur-tarika. Many of us suffer," Gill adds.

How MILS Can Have a Positive Impact on the Health of Women

Mothers-in-law have a significant impact on whether or not women opt for appropriate healthcare. It's not just important to understand the role of the MIL but also target them to activate relevant and critical healthcare options for women. This holds true for both rural and urban women.

While the mother-in-law/daughter-in-law relationship is important in its own right, some studies suggest that the quality of this relationship affects women's well-being and the quality of other relationships. In South Asia,** daughters-in-law with poor relationships with

*https://vc.bridgew.edu/cgi/viewcontent.cgi?article=2676&context=jiws

**https://www.ncbi.nlm.nih.gov/pmc/articles/PMC4852487/

their mothers-in-law are more likely to experience depression.

Dr YK Sandhya, assistant coordinator of the NGO Sahyog, with expertise in maternal health, rights, and sexual health, said to a media network,* "To an extent, we have seen this trend. It is true that MILs try to control their DIL's sexuality. They play a critical role in deciding how many children should be born, how often children should be born. There is no doubt about it because patriarchy is a very strong feature of our Indian society. MILs do influence choice of contraceptives."

She added, "We need to focus on measures that can change the way MILs think."

And so, having seen, heard, and perhaps lived through these experiences, Sameera and her saasu ma have started a social media show called *Sassy Saasuma and Messy Mama* to bust myths and make light of situations. They talk about their relationship, how they navigate life, difficult moments, and fun times.

Positive ties between mothers-in-law and daughters-in-law would reinforce the joint family system.

Pop Culture Portrayal

Devi or dayan—that's the binary trope on Indian television when it comes to the saasu ma or daughter-in-law. The famous Lalita Pawar in India's film industry has epitomised the mother-in-law who permanently

---

*https://www.news18.com/news/india/saas-bahu-and-social-networks-how-a-mother-in-law-influences-a-rural-indian-womans-personal-and-family-well-being-2413439.html

plotted against the bahus of the house. There have been many versions of Pawar since, whether it's Apara Mehta as Savita Virani on the show *Kyunki Saas Bhi Kabhi Bahu Thi*, or Sudha Chandran as Ramola Sikand of *Kahin Kissi Roz*.

"Women like to see their favourite characters express their own feelings, so the mother-in-law identifies with the mother-in-law, the daughter-in-law with the daughter-in-law," is how Ekta Kapoor explained* the surge of soap operas in India.

Even now, in several shows on television, daughters-in-law are generally characterised as relatively powerless women who suffer domination, criticism, and abuse at the hands of their mothers-in-law.

There are some signs that this is changing but not for the majority of India. The rise of web series and other on-demand platforms like Netflix has been instrumental in people exploring new plots and portrayals. Shows with strong and dystopian female characters are injecting a sense of real in how women are projected, and accepted with their flaws and realities. It's not that the MIL-DIL relationship is explored on Over The Top platforms as such, but a few interesting, out-of-the-box portrayals on these new platforms might also help to dismantle stereotypes and introduce less tired, new ways of looking at this age-old contentious relationship. Hopefully that would filter down to regular shows on television and in cinema, too, creating impactful, realistic ways of working through traditional roles.

---

*https://www.nytimes.com/2012/12/26/arts/television/indian-soap-operas-ruled-by-mothers-in-law.html *chapter six*

Bechari, Badass or Bitch

Pop Culture and Women

The prestigious prize for direction in global cinema, Palme D'Or, has only been won by women twice. In 2021, 37-year-old Julia Ducournau marked only the second time in history that a woman director has won one of global cinema's most esteemed prizes, and for the first time alone. The first one was won by Jane Campion, though shared with a male director. This, since the inception of the award in 1955.

Here, the Sahitya Akademi Award, one of the top literary awards of India, has also been accused of biased gender representation. Since 1955, the Akademi has conferred annual awards on the "best" literary works in several languages across four regional zones. According to research by Suraj Jacob and Vanamala Viswanatha published in *Economic and Political Weekly,* "The distribution of Sahitya Akademi Awards shows the fairly predictable pattern of gender gaps. Starting from

1955, and across two dozen languages, less than one-tenth of all awards have gone to women."

Awarded annually to recognise intellectual achievement and academic, cultural, and scientific advances, the Nobel Prize has been bestowed upon more than 900 individuals in the course of its history from 1901 to 2019. Only 53 of the winners have been women, 19 in the categories of physics, chemistry, and physiology or medicine. Marie Curie became the first female laureate in 1903, when she and her husband won a joint prize for physics. Eight years later she was solely awarded the Chemistry Prize, making her the only woman in history to win the Nobel Prize twice. Although women have been behind a number of scientific discoveries throughout history, just 30% of researchers worldwide and 35% of all students enrolled in STEM-related fields of study are women.

If we are a product of what we read, what we see, then clearly patriarchal power structures have been deciding what makes "merit" and what's powerful visualisation or the definition of strong characters. Women's representation in popular culture facilitates the stereotype of the "good" woman who is a simple-minded, emotional, and domesticated female or the outspoken "bad" woman who is either a rebel to be tamed or a home-breaker. This is perpetuated through various forms of media, including movies, cartoons, and television.

"Without the power to define our interests and to participate in the decisions that affect us, women—like any other group in society—will be subject to the definitions and decisions of others." Margaret Marshment in a chapter in the book *Introducing*

Women's Studies calls* pop culture highly political. She notes how men are likely to produce definitions and decisions that serve their own interests and how this need not be a deliberate process of oppression: "It may just seem to be 'common sense' that women should have babies and cook, that women cannot be company directors or bricklayers, that they should wish to totter around on high heels to make themselves attractive to men. This appears to be the natural order of things. So it just happens, 'naturally', that men are spared the drudgery of domestic chores, can have most of the best jobs, and status and wealth that go with them, and can expect women to want to please and service them."

She adds that the way in which women are projected in a subordinate position happens across a multiplicity of structures, institutions, and value systems all of which interact with each other to "lock women into an overall subordination".

Among these lies everything** that is aimed at

---

*https://link.springer.com/chapter/10.1007/978-1-349-25726-3_6

**https://books.google.co.in/books?id=_kxdDwAAQBAJ&pg=PA126&lpg=PA126&dq=%22women+are+depicted+in+ways+that+define+what+it+means+to+be+a+woman+in+this+society:+what+women+are+like+(naturally),+what+they+ought+to+be+like,+what+they%22&source=bl&ots=4zipnaK3pF&sig=ACfU3U3Ty2ApB31qO7E4FHlMK8flf3jXTQ&hl=en&sa=X&ved=2ahUKEwiJit2TsdD3AhW0W3wKHaM5BR0Q6AF6BAgDEAM#v=onepage&q=%22women%20are%20depicted%20in%20ways%20that%20define% 20what%20it%20means%20to%20be% 20a%20woman%20in%20this%20society%3A%20what%20women%20are%20like%20(naturally)%2C%20what%20they%20ought%20to%20be%20like%2C%20what%20they%22&f=false

producing representations of women: from school syllabus to films, from advertising to opera, from game shows, books, book awards to art galleries, women are depicted in ways that define what it means to be a woman in this society: what women are like (naturally), what they ought to be like, what they are capable of, and incapable of, what roles they play in society, and how they differ from men.

While portrayal is central to the problem, what's also problematic is how we recognise, celebrate or reward women in these spaces. Take, for example, some of the awards we talked about above or even the globally acclaimed Man Booker Prize.

An artificial intelligence-based analysis of the prestigious Man Booker Prize was done by IBM, and it revealed bias and stereotyping in the writings based on features like occupation, introductions, and actions associated with the characters in the book.

A report by media house QZ on the analysis noted male characters were described with terms such as "rich", "handsome", and "strong", while women were identified mainly as "beautiful", "lovely", "pretty", or "romantic". Not just that, men in these books held more prominent jobs like doctors, professors, novelists, directors, and priests. Female characters were mainly described as a "teacher" or a "whore." Things are on the mend but far from showing a trend. The 2022 International Booker Prize was won by *Tomb of Sand*, written by Geetanjali Shree and translated by Daisy Rockwell. The winning book is called *Ret Samadhi* in Hindi, which is located in north India and revolves around the life of an 80-year-old widow. The protagonist is searching for herself, her roots, and navigating a relationship with her daughter. The book, therefore, breaks barriers not just in terms of who picked the Booker prize but also the characterisation of women and normalising the need to capture stories of older women.

Consuming more works by women is a way of balancing your understanding of the world that pop culture creates. Being a journalist, I have always recognised that there is a discerning distinction in the voices of men and women when they direct, perform or write. We share the same world but we live our lives by a different set of norms, governed by our gender. It is but natural that our gaze towards the world is different.

But the fact that we have not captured storytelling through the lens of women has led to deep repercussions on how women are viewed, what opportunities they get, and the mind space their works capture.

India's massive film industry, collectively called Bollywood, is to blame for why women in India have been relegated to gender-specific roles in society, at home, on screen.

"The massiveness of Hindi film industry the so called Bombay cinema, and its wide popularity have a particular significance for cultural politics in India... emerged as an essential factor in the formation of the social self-image and behaviour," says Reeta Chowdhary Tremblay in her paper* titled *Representation and reflection of self and society in Bombay cinema.*

---

*https://www.tandfonline.com/doi/abs/10.1080/09584939608719798?journalCode=ccsa20

But as author Jaya Misra says* "In TV, especially in soaps, we have this unsaid formula—badjalan ladki (shameless girl) and bechari ladki (naïve girl). The badjalan will always lose, bechari will always win."

She adds, "The badjalan will have all the spunk in her, while the bechari has all the goody-goody characteristics... She's the person who will never flirt, who is always going to be a virgin even after she gets married...she will never have a wedding night..."

Television, as separate from cinema, is a very popular mode of entertainment across India. Which means it has its own sets of demands in terms of TRP and the limit to which content and characters can be modernised.

But even if directors or actors can try to rewrite history, and try to stop portraying stereotypical characters, they have to battle against the grain. Shikha Makan, who wrote India's version of *Ugly Betty*, *Jassi Jaissi Koi Nahin*, says she had to fight to keep Jassi's character different.

She said,** "The ideas behind that show were very progressive and it was very interesting to write. Here we were creating a character, though inspired from a foreign show, who had her own sense of agency, despite not being in the description of what makes a great successful woman on screen, as TV had defined it forever—sanskari, very beautiful, a head turner. Jassi was odd, yet she had so much inner strength and

---

*https://www.shethepeople.tv/news/struggles-in-changing-the-prototype-of-female-characterisation/

**https://www.shethepeople.tv/news/struggles-in-changing-the-prototype-of-female-characterisation/

the capacity to assert herself, and that set her out. It was a defining moment on Indian TV after Tara. But as things were progressing and the time was coming closer to transform her, all the ideas of using the same old gaze of men come into play. That is when I began to have fights and left the show." Eventually Jassi's character had to be given a complete makeover to appear beautiful in the most conventional sense.

There is a strong tradeoff between writing shows and films that are questioning the stereotype and those which can bring in strong ratings. If done correctly, the audience does swallow a dose of progressive writing with copious amounts of drama. But it's tough.

Ashvini Yardi, who was part of the production of a controversial program, *Balika Vadhu* (child marriage) in India says, Bollywood "basically runs on hero culture". The program, which ran over 2000 episodes, revolves around the life of a child bride transitioning from her childhood to womanhood.

"It is a great idea, to tell the truth in the drama of a lie. So you tell what you have to, but you also give it that drama, otherwise people won't accept it," says Yardi about programs with a social message.

In India, over 800 feature films are produced annually and around 7.5 million people go to permanent and temporary theatres daily in a non-pandemic year. Over 350 million people consume content on OTT platforms. The huge viewership and fandom of Bollywood clearly corroborates its impact on the discourse, gender dynamics, and perception of people in the society. But the question that we need to ask is whether the influence of pop culture on society is right or not? Does Bollywood deliver the right perception of gender, especially women, to our society that is predominantly male-dominated? Does the representation of women in Indian cinema address the issue of gender inequality or does it worsen it?

According to a 2017 report[*] by Geena Davis Institute on Women in Media supported by UN Women and the Rockefeller Foundation, Indian films topped the list when it came to objectifying women on the screens. Since the inception of Indian cinema, women have been rendered as props, decorative objects, supporting roles, victims, martyrs or becharis.

The Male Gaze

Indian films are made from the vision of a typical cis-gender heterosexual man. Not just that, the audiences are also considered to be predominantly heterosexual males. So, filmmakers build stories from a male point of view, with an inclination to objectify and sexualise women.

The focus of the camera on the body, dance moves of women, and their perception through a lens of male desire and the male gaze do an injustice to the representation of women as individuals with agency. It undermines their capability as an actor, glorifies gender inequality and deepens the gender divide already present in society.

"Men look at women. Women watch themselves being looked at. This determines not only most relations

* https://seejane.org/wp-content/uploads/cinema-and-society-investigation-of-the-impact-on-gender-representation-in-indian-films.pdf

between men and women but also the relation of women to themselves," John Berger in his book, *Ways of Seeing** writes. "The surveyor of women in herself is male: the surveyed female. Thus she turns herself into an object—and most particularly an object of vision: a sight."

Filmmaker Prakash Jha says that the portrayal of the ideal woman in cinema is from the "male perspective" and he notes that it comes in many different ways, and cites four types of the male gaze. The germination of the plot is the first but Jha adds that the gaze of the camera and all that it reveals about the woman to the audience is also a kind of male gaze. The third is the male character's response to the woman on screen and, lastly, the response of the men in the audience to the woman on the screen.

Jha, speaking to newswire *IANS* said that all of these factors ultimately culminate into the influence that cinema may have on gender equality. He also lamented the abysmally low ratio of women in the Indian film industry and pointed out that their voices are, therefore, not being heard.

"One has to understand how small the representation of women in cinema is. Every aspect of filmmaking, from the stories to the camera and onto direction, is dominated by the males," he notes.

Does this come from a deep sense of how our society perceives women?

Malayalam film actor, Jewel Mary, grew up near

---

*https://onartandaesthetics.com/2017/01/12/john-berger-on-male-and-female-presence-from-ways-of-seeing/

Kochi in the Indian southern state of Kerala. She was tall and brown and was kept out of all the games about princesses and bridesmaids because she didn't fit in. "I was too tall, and too dark, with no doll-like figure and had a strong voice.

"I was told I would never succeed in my life with this dark skin. To get a career, be successful and find a good guy to marry I would need to become fairer."

Growing up, she was compared with her sister who is fairer than her, crushing her confidence. Mary was mocked for wanting to be an actor because women on screen came with a prescription for how they must look. This led to a significant amount of "self loathing" she says.

Even her mother was conditioned by generations of beliefs about "how" women should be. Mary adds, "She is a victim. She has heard these things through her generation. She told me to lighten my skin and look better."

"I was told to try injections on my face to sculpt it or lighten the skin, I was asked to use foundation colours lighter than my own skin," she says.

It was so deeply internalised—this sense of what she was not—that broad-shouldered Mary was forced to take up roles as "a man" on stage as a "defence mechanism". "In a way it gave me power and strength to break those stereotypes." She took up portrayals of the anti-hero, of a villain, to be noticed for her talent.

"We don't identify uniqueness in our culture. We identify those with something different as 'outsiders', those who are excluded."

Jewel Mary's story is symptomatic of how India's

film industry shapes the thinking of how we portray and treat women. On screen and in reality.

A woman's physical appearance is directly related to the opportunities she gets. Actor Tisca Chopra, who directed a film, *Rubaroo*, inspired by Meryl Streep, talks of ageism in our film industry. "After a certain age you are termed dignified and central parts dry up for you. Just when you are at the peak of your performing powers."

Chopra's film on the sensitive issue of ageism comes at a time when Indian society is raising pertinent questions about women claiming their rights and spaces. In Bollywood, for the longest time, perhaps even as recently until 2014, actresses would hide their marriage or pregnancies. But today they are out loud and proud talking about motherhood and are marrying at the peak of their careers. Nearly all top actors from Kareena Kapoor Khan, Deepika Padukone, and Alia Bhatt are married.

Representation of Women in Cinema

Starting from the 60s and 70s, representation of women in Indian cinema has been across two extremes. They are either the abla naaris, homely women, sacrificial mothers or victims at the mercy of the villains or heroes. Or they are vamps who are seen as promiscuous and live with the edgy bad guy, automatically translating them into "bad women".

Movies like *Sangam* (1964) and *Jai Santoshi Maa* (1975), among others, depicted women in traditional roles that Indian audiences aspired to have in their own houses. These movies played around the narrative of a typical "good woman" who is sacrificial, bears all oppressions at the hands of both men and women and, at last, her perseverance bears fruit and movie ends with a happily-ever-after glorifying both the traditional and sacrificial nature of women, and the masculinity of the man who acts as the saviour.

What is the reason behind this bias or divide in the representation of actors on screen? Is this divide a representation of the society that we inhabit? And is change somewhere around the corner?

Although some movies did try to break the mould by focusing the camera on women, they still remained within the boundaries of patriarchal perception of women. For example, the movie *Mother India* is a phenomenal example of a women-centric movie where the focus, narrative, and climax revolved around Nargis Dutt. It was perhaps for the first time that women were perceived as the strength and honour of the country and even an embodiment of it. But then again, the movie glorified the role of sacrificial "good" mothers in opposition to the mothers who are career-oriented and prioritise themselves along with the welfare of the kids. Another very prominent example of the "good mother" narrative is the movie *Karan Arjun* that released much later in 1995.

This reinforced the fact that Indian audiences fantasise about sacrificial mothers while "villainising" those who are not as selfless. An example of this binary is Preity Zinta in *Kabhi Alvida Na Kehna* who appears in the role of a career-oriented mother who prioritises her career along with motherhood. But she has been shown as a "bad mother" who is not as sacrificial and selfless as Rakhi in *Karan Arjun* or Nargis Dutt in *Mother India*. This might not have been the director's intention but it is a fact that after her husband leaves, she is shown as participating actively in her son's life.

Moreover, although Basanti in *Sholay* (1975)—an iconic film which is still watched by every Indian even remotely invested in Bollywood—came forward as the strong bread earner of the family, by the end of the film she was rendered a damsel in distress who is at the mercy of the goodness of Gabbar or the masculinity of her lover Veeru. Jaya Bachchan was nothing more than the widowed love interest of Jay played by Amitabh Bachchan.

Another major problem with the movies of this era is the idea of defining womanhood in terms of nationalism. Women were depicted as the embodiment of a pure and sacred country, Bharat mata, which needs to be preserved by manpower. This alignment of women with the country not only justifies her objectification or dismissal of her individuality, but also draws a limit on her agency over her life. Depicting women as the embodiment of the country only added inertia to the narrow and patriarchal ideas of woman's morality.

Representation of Women in the 80s and 90s

Even when we look at the women characters in the movies of the 80s and 90s, they were not more than the love interests of the heroes—his sister, damsel in distress, or a seductress. In the movie *Hum* released in 1991, Tiger, played by Big B, saves Juma Gonsalves, played by Kimi Katkar, whose role transforms from damsel in distress to the love interest of the hero who is valourised for his benevolent sexism. In this era, what also became prominent was rape narratives. Women were frequently depicted as victims of rape and their victimisation and passivity was then used to boost the masculinity of the hero. One of the favourite rape narratives of Hindi cinema of this age was the rape of the hero's sister which enraged him and turned him from a timid and gay character to a revengeful hero. Examples of this narrative were seen in movies like *Aaghaz*, *Shola Aur Shabnam*, *Aaj Ki Aawaz*, among others. In *Shola Aur Shabnam*, Govinda's playful character suddenly undergoes a transformation when his sister is stripped in public by the villain.

Even though the representation of rape on screen marked a significant move from aspirational mode to realistic mode of the Hindi film, it could not give women their agency. Women still had no voice, no freedom to exercise their rights and were dependent on men for their safety and needs. The rape narratives, even though they reflected the reality of the society, did not allow women to take action, rendered her as the silent bechari waiting for a man to save her and make her realise her worth.

Such movies exacerbated the rape culture prevelant in the society by making rape and rescue of a woman a symbol of masculinity. It will not be wrong to say that Bollywood in its 90s has played a significant role in romanticising eve teasing, stalking and trivialising a woman's "no" since its inception.

Representation of Women in the 2000s

The hope for better representation of women in a decade that saw major developments in the country, only led to more disappointment. So as India was progressing in technology and liberalisation, our portrayal of women in pop culture was becoming more and more trivial. This was the age where women characters were mainly decorative and eve-teasing was romanticised, adding to the rape culture prevalent in our society. An example of a movie glorifying stalking as an expression of love would be *Raanjhanaa* released in 2013.

Not only in the 2000s but in the 50s to 90s too, stalking and women's unclear consent was used as a prop in romantic stories. This again is a major medium to reduce women's agency and impose male desire under the garb of love and protection. The reflection of this is seen in the real world where every other woman would agree about being stalked or eve-teased many times in her life. "Eve-teasing", a term coined in India, is when a man makes unsolicited advances on the road to entice a woman. It is today one of the prevailing silent crimes against women in India because they are rarely reported as Bollywood has normalised it in the minds of both men and women.

Even the on-screen representation of women's nudity saw an increase in this era. A 2017 Geena Davis report stated, "Indian women are three times more likely than men to be portrayed with some nudity (35% compared to 13.5%). They are also three times more likely to appear in revealing clothing than men (34.1% compared to 12.2%)." The nudity, scantily dressed seductresses, and item songs which pervaded Hindi cinema from the 90s to 2000s was the inevitable result of the impact of western culture on Indian pop culture. Although Fatima Shareek, in her article "Western Influence on Bollywood"* states that Bollywood was "a rip off of Hollywood" since the 50s, it will not be wrong to say that the western tradition of "Rock and Roll" and skimpy, tight outfits became more popular between the 80s and 2000s.

Moreover, what also explains the western influence on Bollywood's representation of women is its obsession with zero size and fair skin. If you remember, in 2008 Kareena Kapoor Khan hit headlines for losing weight and attaining a size-zero figure. She appeared in the movie *Tashan* in which, according to me, her role vacillated between being a love interest of the heroes and an eye candy for the audience because of her figure and apparels. The Geena Davis report cited the impact of this obsession with thin bodies by stating, "Reported cases of eating disorders have increased over five times since 1990 as Indian media has become more Westernized, and previous research has linked this to unattainable standards of beauty put forth in entertainment media."

On the other hand, the obsession with fair-skinned women is not a new story, whether it is on screen or off screen. The brilliant example of the trope is in the movie *Vivaah* where the younger sister, whose skin is dark, is often shamed while Poonam, played by Amrita

*https://medium.com/@fshareef345/western-influence-on-bollywood-b293580045ba

Rao, is glorified for her fairness. And more often than not, characters of lower caste are represented with darker skin in Bollywood, a phenomenon now known as brownface in Bollywood. But we still cannot seem to understand that our beauty standards, which are based on the binaries of fair and dark, are a colonial hangover. We are still reeling under the impact of colonisation because the glorification of fair skin is an idea borrowed from our colonisers.

Lesser Screen Time, Lesser Dialogues: Women Lack Agency in Reel and Real Life

Statistically, women occupy a lot less screen time compared to male actors. Other than the fact that men have been portrayed in powerful roles of leaders, saviours, tycoons, and as the epitome of success and fame, women rarely get the opportunity to grace such roles onscreen. Women often also get fewer dialogues than men.

India produces the highest number of films in the world. The Indian box office is valued at multi-billion dollars. Despite the scale and cultural impact of cinema in the country, there is little credible documentation on women in film.

A research named “O Womaniya” by Ormax Media and Film Companion stated that men get 81% of the dialogues in trailers while women get only 19%.

All 129 films included in the survey were evaluated on the Bechdel Test, which is an internationally-accepted measure of female representation in cinema. For a film to pass the Bechdel Test, it must satisfy the following condition: There is at least one scene in the film in which two named female characters are having a conversation that's not about a man/men. Most Bollywood blockbusters failed.

Taapsee Pannu, who is one of the most dependable actors of Hindi cinema noted, "In my early years in the movies, I was once asked to change my dialogues during the dub because the hero wanted it altered. I refused to do it, only to find out after the release of the film, that they had gone ahead and got another dubbing artist to voice my bits there." Later she would tell me how often producers would try to convince her to accept a lower cheque than the actor.

Women are "still underrepresented" on screen, noted a Nielsen* diversity report on TV in America. Women make up 52% of the US population—but are visible on screen only 38% of the time.

The lack of dialogues of women characters is significant to conclude that women lack agency on the screen. Similarly, in the real world, men out-talk women. Birmingham Young University Political Science Professor Jessica R. Preece** says, "Women are systematically seen as less authoritative. And their influence is systematically lower. And they're speaking less. And when they're speaking up, they're not being listened to as much, and they are being interrupted more."

---

*https://www.usatoday.com/story/entertainment/tv/2020/12/03/diversity-television-women-less-represented-according-nielsen/3792406001/

**https://magazine.byu.edu/article/when-women-dont-speak/

Women vs Women

Aren't we so done with this scene—one woman takes on the other and there is a fight and everyone sits around and enjoys it. So many of us have seen this in our own homes. So many have wondered why it must be so. The saas-bahu dramas and films have deeply established women as rivals of each other. Or where they are in a triangle vying for one man as jealous rivals. In fact, in almost all plots, the blame of an affair is put on another woman.

There is no narrative of sisterhood and women are not seen as each others' enablers.

A Wave of Change: But Gradual

In the last few years, India's otherwise male-dominated "dabangg" (boisterous) film industry, has experimented with many progressive projects fronted by men and women and found business sense in it. By that one means that a hit-obsessed Bollywood, wanting to only cast heroes who deliver 100 crore rupees at the box office, are finally waking up to other ways of creating content, and making money.

What's added to this momentum is the power of the web-series and Over The Top (OTT) platforms that are welcoming brave and breakthrough content that shows a mirror to society. *Article 15*, led by Ayushmann Khurrana was a successful movie focussed on the disappearance of young girls due to caste-based oppression. Some other must-mentions are *Chandigarh Kare Aashqui*, which was an unconventional story about a man falling in love with a transwoman. *Badhaai Ho* questioned stereotypes about a woman having a child in her middle age and dealing with social repercussions of a late pregnancy. A series titled *Bombay Begums* spotlighted menopausal woman and reflected on real-life situations women across ages face.

These streaming platforms are also helping mainstream excellent content in other languages to wider audiences. Notable works like the Malayalam film called *Sara*, about a woman who didn't want a baby, *Great Indian Kitchen* which spoke about the burden of household duties falling on women and even *Uyare*, which focussed on the life of an acid attack survivor who wants to realise her dreams.

It was not just men who were driving the narrative in these innovative plots and they did well, and attracted audiences.

Vidya Balan, the heroine who has become the "hero" of her films, has done many significant feature films where she is the lead. This is a general breakthrough from the past, where women have been the love-interest of the main star, a strong male character. "I love playing roles of women who have aspirations and dreams of their own and who overcome all sorts of hurdles to realise those dreams," says Balan, who played the role of the mathematician Shakuntala Devi, called the Human Super Computer.

But growing into the industry, Balan hardly escaped the pressure. "The gender pay gap is huge," she adds. And no matter who you want to grow up to be, you are cast with a stereotypical view and expected to deliver more than your job. Balan shares how her mother would always ask her to learn cooking. She would then respond by saying that she would hire a cook or marry a man who knows how to cook.

At the bottom of this, like for many other women, is the fact that we read, watch, and imbibe gendered roles around women.

But like Balan's roles, in the past few years, a wave of change has ruffled the red carpets of Bollywood. Women directors like Zoya Akhtar, Alankrita Shrivastava and women actors and producers like Priyanka Chopra Jonas, Anushka Sharma, Deepika Padukone, Konkona Sen Sharma, and Vidya Balan, amongst others, have proved that women alone can carry the entire movie on their shoulders. Movies like *Mary Kom, Lipstick Under My Burkha, Sherni, Bulbul,* and more have women characters in the lead. Their role is much beyond their mention as co-lead in the movie credits and often breaks the gendered standards set by the 80-year-long history of Bollywood.

Alankrita Shrivastava's film, *Lipstick Under My Burkha*, was banned in India for being "lady-oriented" with bold female characters. The film soared at global festivals, creating worldwide curiosity, forcing Indian authorities to eventually lift the ban. Helmed by four female actors, stuck in their own ruts headlined by patriarchal restrictions, the film portrayed an older woman's sexual desires, a burkha-wearing wife who suffered rape by her husband, an aspiring local parlour-wali beautician and a female tailor whose parents wouldn't let her live a regular teen's life. The film picked international awards and accolades from audiences. It filled an important gap in cinema viewing.

"Indian cinema has really been moulded by men for decades now," says Shrivastava. "Even the form of cinema has been totally shaped by men. We don't even know what it would be like when more women tell their stories in mainstream cinema."

She further added, "Our societies just don't like the idea of free women."

Many filmmakers are positive about the steady yet remarkable shift in the representation of women in pop culture. "The line between the heroine and the vamp has blurred. This is a perfect example of diminishing stereotypes. It's a welcome sign that the films are trying to outgrow the set pattern of demarcating the characters. Films such as *Mary Kom, Kahaani* or *Haider*—where Tabu is depicted as an atypical filmi mother—have been appreciated by the audience. This is a clear proof that the audience wants our films to break away from stereotypes," said ad filmmaker Prahlad Kakkar* in *India Today*. While documentary filmmaker and media professor, Shohini Ghosh,** says in an interview "Film has its own language in which silence can be as eloquent as speech...I personally feel much is changing especially with the advent of streaming platforms which show great diversity in the representation of genders and sexuality."

It is undeniable that pop culture plays a vital role in formulating our opinions and perspectives. The

---

*https://www.indiatoday.in/movies/bollywood/story/depicting-women-in-bollywood-222702-2014-10-11

**https://timesofindia.indiatimes.com/home/sunday-times/in-bollywood-women-get-screen-time-but-very-little-talk-time/articleshow/81608541.cms influence of pop culture is not restricted to copying the hairstyle of the hero or heroine but expands to envisioning their reality.

In Tamil Nadu, over the last few years, there's been the rise of a rapper movement that questions caste, class, and other stereotypes women face. Arivarasu Kalainesan, more commonly known as Arivu, is an Indian rapper who, in his song *Thamizhachi*, has tried to celebrate the "audacity" and arrogance of a woman. In an interview with *Edex*, Arivu says, "It's easy to get famous with a song criticising women. I didn't want that sort of easy fame, I want to write for women as well and talk about how they don't need anyone to determine their freedom. Whether they want to go to a pub, drink or smoke, they cannot be criticised."

Feminism today has become a capitalist agenda, some would argue. Pop culture, media, and advertising wave the flag of feminism and women empowerment only to encash it by attracting a certain demographic of women. But the question is, do the films or media that portray women empowerment and feminism really stand by it? Or is it a great load of pinkwashing?

Pointing out that the shift in the narrative of women on screen is gradual and still there is much to be done, Paromita Vohra, filmmaker and founder of Agents of Ishq says in an interview on *SheThePeople*, we need to look at pop culture beyond film, and include social media, web series, short formats, and even TikTok and the world of many different languages. "So when we say popular culture we must include all of these. Unfortunately all of the conversation online tends to cherry pick only say—five movies—and then it's common to say item numbers are bad and so is objectification. This is a kind of undergraduate level of understanding."

She adds, India has seen a greater segmentation of gender and greater gendering. "Films about women are only to do with women and films about queer people are only about queer people while films that are only about men or have a masculine protagonist become general films about everybody. A world of cinema with all kinds of characters and different spaces given to different people in different ways has become harder," says Vohra* in another interview.

The thing with pop culture is that it's so widespread, that any change is very gradual. We shouldn't forget that change in films and social media isn't driven by what is right but what is liked by audiences.

Whether or not these movies become blockbusters is besides the point. They have started an important movement to showcase powerful roles and representation of women on the screen. Until audiences experience a change in the perception and see women as strong leads on screen, it will never get normalised.

---

*https://timesofindia.indiatimes.com/home/sunday-times/in-bollywood-women-get-screen-time-but-very-little-talk-time/articleshow/81608541.cms *chapter seven*

A Healthy Girl

Gopal has four daughters, each a year apart. The younger three were born trying for a boy. The family lives in a small village in Uttar Pradesh and practice farming. For about half the year, Gopal has a job as a guard in a small community. As the only earning member of his family he doesn't make enough for the girls to be educated and Gopal's main goal is to save to get the girls married.

The situation of women in India is alarming because we worship them as goddesses on one hand and burn them for dowry on the other. India reports 24 dowry deaths a day. A rape every 15 minutes. And these are only the reported statistics.

Women are raised to be "given away" in marriage. As a result, the investment in their health and wellbeing is never a priority because they belong to a different household eventually. A World Bank report for 2012 titled "Gender Equality and Development" notes how change comes slowly or "not at all" for women.

Covering the last three decades, the report particularly picks "health disadvantages" as an outcome of a society where social norms give more power, attention and, responsibility to men and leave women without agency to make choices, have rights, or express desires across age groups.

We also look at women's health in silos. Many women talk about how their first check-up happens once they are pregnant. What's also problematic is the belief that the only healthcare women need is gynaecological—collectively termed "ladies problems" in Indian society.

Mem Arora had just announced her first pregnancy after a year of marriage. The Arora family, based in Phagwara in Punjab, was elated and festivities were announced all around, from luxury mithai boxes for friends to cash pouch "shaguns" being given to the expecting mother. "At one such party, Aunty Raj Oberoi came and sat next to me to discuss the sex of the child," recounts Arora. In Punjab, for most families the spends on festivities and baby showers are directly proportional to the sex of the child. "She gave me a pouch of 'homemade' capsules that would ensure I had a baby boy." Arora, though shocked, was teased by the family to take it and told "'What's the harm, it's Ayurvedic and homemade." Arora didn't take the capsules, backed by her military husband, and produced two daughters. The family leaves no occasion to remind her about not having taken those capsules.

From aunties peddling desi nuskas (local homemade medicines and therapies) to relegating women's health needs to what other women think or do, has meant that women themselves have given up on seeking professional healthcare unless the situation gets dire and she needs to be hospitalised.

A cultural problem with this is how little women can talk about health in the open. It nearly never makes it to the dining table conversations, for example. This is also because of the complete absence of women in nutrition and health advertisements and media, outside of pregnancy needs. For example, Indian ads have forever glorified hiding sanitary napkins. "Chup chup baithe ho jaroor koi baat hai," was one ad jingle which basically teased a girl for sitting quietly in a corner while others were playing throwball and she was stuck because of her period. "Sshhhh" has been the central storyline of media talking about pads (which has been the universe of all things women for decades, relegating all of women's needs to that piece of processed cotton paper), and that meant that the chemist around the corner would wrap sanitary napkins in brown paper or an opaque black packet.

Fifty-six-year-old Prabha Jain blames herself for raising her daughters to believe periods were a shame. "I would show big eyes to my girls when the period ads would come and signal them to leave the room 'to get some water'. I never really cared whether their father was embarrassed but my internal conditioning was so severe I would ensure my girls came back to the room only after a few ads had passed or when they had 'finished getting a glass of water'." Jain's story is the story of nearly every Indian household. And the sanitary napkin incidents can be extrapolated to every health discussion. It's the 2020s, and many of us in urban India think this is a conversation from the 80s but no, it's the truth of our "now". Indeed, we are questioning these in some moments of excitement and activism, but broadly, a large part of India is still shy and ashamed of women's "problems".

Jitender Singh, who lives in a town near Jalandhar, is a proud patriarch and the owner of many farms. His son is studying to leave for Canada, which is the ambition of nearly every other young man in the state of Punjab. As per data out in 2020, there was a 400% increase in the trend amongst youth for migrating to Canada from India, and Punjabis constituted 60% of the migration to Canada.

For women in Punjab, the forced goals are marriage or being "exported" to America where they are often married to taxi drivers and shop owners. There are thousands of cases where such marriages end in horrific cases of—and not without enough evidence—domestic violence. Whether the affluent or the middle class, there is a stark discomfort discussing girls and women and their health.

"Girls should be girls," Singh said to me when we got into a conversation about raising his daughters to become sportswomen because a lot of girls from Patiala get into national sports. It's not that he doesn't know how modern views are fast changing and women are fighting for an equal field. "But we have been raised like this, and I cannot change." He is also very amused that girls today are beginning to consume bone strengthening capsules, and there is a special "Bournvita" (standard term for malt extract health drinks in India) targeted at women. What he says next really seems to be the crux of the issue. "Women should be graceful and delicate, not strong and muscular."

On one side there are cultural issues. And then there are circumstances.

In 2020, while writing this book, I travelled the vast breadth of Uttarakhand. On one such occasion I met teenage girls huddled around a hand pump, washing buckets full of clothes. Rani, who is 14, says she had to drop out of school to help the family with chores. "All the young girls of this village typically study till class five or six and then our parents need us to help them out. More hands means less work for one person." Rani comes around noon, after helping out with work at home, with a large bucket of unwashed garments. Along with four other girls they wash clothes, chat and return home in an hour or so.

What are the factors that force women to stay home and ignore their wellbeing as a whole by starting to work in the family too early—in both rural and urban families?

The most obvious is expectations of domesticity and that's across urban and rural landscapes because it really depends on how willing families are to send their girls to school. Safety of girls travelling alone to school itself is a big reason why—at least in small villages—girls are held back. Seema Samridhi, is a firebrand lawyer who fought the case for Nirbhaya, a term the Indian government gave to the girl who was gangraped in 2012 in a moving bus, leading to global attention on India's safety norms for women. Samridhi was born in a home of four daughters and really lobbied with her parents to let her go to school. "I had to cross a forest to reach school and my parents were always so worried for my safety that they would rather I didn't go. But I persisted." Women are routinely eve-teased (a term popular in India for boys taunting or teasing women on the road with sexual remarks) on the way to colleges but are afraid to tell their parents, for that could well mean they would prevent them from attending school if they complained. All of these reasons play into women de-prioritising themselves across the board. What starts with falling behind in the education curve, reflects on the health and nutrition curve.

It is not a surprise that men are healthier than women. Women are expected to invest their time and effort in taking care of the welfare of their family members while ignoring their own health. One of the major factors behind this is the value given to women's presence in the house throughout the day. It is not common in our society for women to take a day off, sleep in, visit a doctor but rather they are expected to cook, serve, and clean daily. Women are expected to be omnipresent to cater to the needs of the family. In such cases, women rarely get the time to think about going for a regular medical check-up or taking rest if they are ill. Women are mainly seen in terms of their labour. They are valued only until they can provide service to the men in the house. And in order to preserve their value and not be replaced by another woman who dedicates herself to unpaid domestic work, women tend to ignore anything that demands attention away from domestic work. When village women are given the power to measure their own health, they ask different questions than the questions that are typically used in research surveys designed by experts. Researchers at the World Bank asked village women in Tamil Nadu to design questions to track their own, and their peers' health and wellbeing. They added a very crucial question, "Has the person who eats last in your family gone hungry in the last week?" This very question suggests that women ignore themselves in favour of everyone else in their families.

Secondly, the idea of male-child preference is deep-rooted in our society. It keeps on spreading and affecting anything that comes in between, especially the wellbeing of women. The vicious cycle begins when families force women to undergo multiple pregnancies just to produce a male child, irrespective of whether the woman's body is capable of those pregnancies or not. Women are seen as vessels of producing children and not as individuals. In our society, it is said that if a woman cannot produce children, especially males, she has no value or reason for existence. As a result, many women force themselves to undergo a spree of pregnancies to prove their worth. Moreover, because of male-child preference, girls in the families are never prioritised when it comes to children's welfare. From receiving the extra half of the milk from the girl child's glass to going for regular medical check-ups, male kids' welfare is considered as the paramount responsibility of the family. In fact, research has also shown that preference for not just male children, but preference for the eldest male child explains why child stunting in India is higher than in poorer regions like sub-Saharan Africa.

This brings me to the next factor that causes

women's health to be ignored—the idea of paraya dhan. Women are perceived as paraya dhan. They have to be married off to another family and so it is assumed that her welfare is the responsibility of the "other family". Families do not find it profitable to invest in the health and wellbeing of daughters as they are not going to stay with them for a long time.

This gender gap in access to medical health has been evident in the studies performed on the number of boys and girls that visit hospitals. A study* shows that women account for only 45% of all hospital visits. Girls under 15 years form only 33% of hospital visits. Moreover, further analysis shows that there are over 2,25,000 missing female hospital visits between 2017 and 2019 for nephrology, cardiology, and oncology care alone.

Even if some families value a woman's health it is only to make sure that their reproductive system is healthy. Even medical research differentiates between male and female bodies based on the reproductive system. All the research on women's bodies, if conducted, is concentrated on their reproductive system, and the rest is dismissed as uninteresting. This is despite the fact that women face chronic pains more frequently and intensely than men. Cardiovascular diseases are the major cause of death among women. Women are at an equal risk of having heart attacks as men and despite this, heart attack is seen as a man's disease. Among women and men who smoke, women are 20–70%

---

*https://www.nber.org/system/files/working_papers/w28972/w28972.pdf

more likely to be affected by lung cancer. Moreover, mental health problems are as common among women as it is among men although the fatality rate is higher among men. The COVID-19 pandemic itself affected women more than men for various reasons.

Jyoti lives in a small village in the Kumaon mountains that houses the world-famous tiger reserve, the Jim Corbett Park. She has two little boys, her husband works in a factory in Delhi and she stays with the larger joint family of 11 members in a big home in the village. Her daily routine includes waking at 6 am, washing the cows, feeding them, and heading out to the farm to till and sow. During one of my meetings with her, I inquired about her general health check-ups and how often she goes to a doctor to get them. "Kabhi bimar padhte hai toh doctor ke paas jaate hain." (We go to the doctor when we fall sick.)

Her first gynaecology check-up and thyroid test was done after she got pregnant. Other than the time she was expecting, she has not gone in for regular check-ups.

Mumbai-based Sudeshna Ray, who is a gynaecologist and medical director of *Gytree*, says, "First of all, they don't consider themselves important. They feel everyone else is important. Women sacrifice their health in taking care of others. Secondly, if somebody else is not asking women to take care of themselves they will not take care. Women feel that if they can take care of their husband, their husband will reciprocate which doesn't happen in most cases. Men do not think in that way. And third is that women are scared that if they go to the doctor they will come up with something they are not ready to face."

But do we even understand what is the outcome of the lack of awareness and attention towards women's health? Do we know that deteriorating women's health impacts the growth of the economy, population, and the country? Do we know that lack of awareness towards women's health has an intergenerational impact too? That if women's health is ignored today, it will affect the workforce, growth, and GDP of tomorrow. And before everything else, why don't we understand that good health is a woman's basic right? Why do we necessarily need an explanation to prioritise women's wellbeing?

In a male-dominated society, it is difficult for people to understand how women's involvement improves almost every sector of society. Women's good health ensures a better literacy rate, growth in the country's economy and GDP, growth in the position of the country globally, and better human capital for the future. Any country that limits women's contribution to society to only childbearing pays a heavy price in terms of its socioeconomic development.

Role of Mothers

Mothers not only care for their children by nurturing, feeding, bathing and clothing them, but also by protecting them. When they are in a position to do so, women also direct household resources to the care and upbringing of their children. Studies in a variety of low-income settings have shown that where women are income earners, they are more likely than men to spend their earnings on goods and services that benefit the household, e.g., food, education, and medicine.

To be more precise, if changes in policies and mindsets of the society are implemented to improve women's health, women's participation in education and employment will also increase. Not only do mothers need health support but they can become the reason why millions of girls prioritise their health.

Mental health was never heard of in Sunita Gupta's life until she was diagnosed with it. Sunita, who lives in Dehri-on-Sone, a small town in Bihar, faced a lot of problems and stigmas to speak up and demand treatment for her illness which was an advanced level of obsessive-compulsive disorder and depression. Her family never thought that women can be affected by mental health disorders or that there was an illness like that. Sunita's husband too took time to understand that his wife needed psychiatric help. But he stood up and provided care and support. Later, when Kamala Gupta was diagnosed with major depression and psychosis, it was her mother, Sunita, who identified the symptoms first and stirred the discussion of seeking psychiatric help for her daughter.

Sunita and Kamla's story tell us that mothers not only should take care of their own bodies and health but also encourage their daughters to seek medical help for any discomfort. It is said that educated and empowered mothers raise empowered daughters; similarly, a mother who is well aware of women's health issues carries the responsibility of educating her daughters about the importance of medical health. It is not a hidden fact that mothers or women generally internalise the lack of importance and awareness about their health. So changing their mindset is crucial to developing a society of healthy women. Mothers are the caregivers. But the caregiving should not be limited to the male members of the family. It should include the mothers themselves and the daughters.

If society prioritises women's health, it will contribute to increasing the literacy rate within a country and on the global index. Healthy women will seek better education opportunities and vice versa. A study shows that 52% of girls in India are absent in schools due to frequent illnesses. The most prominent illness among girls in India is related to the lack of menstruation hygiene. Twenty-three million women in India drop out of school when they begin menstruating.

Apart from menstruation, other chronic health problems affect women more than men because of the prevalent male-child preference culture in our society. Studies have shown how female patients are missing in healthcare centres. The ratio of male to female patients in states like Bihar is as high as 2.37. In 2016, out of 2 lakh patients in AIIMS Delhi, male patients visited hospitals 1.69 times more than female patients.

Furthermore, many studies have shown that educated and employed women push the country towards a better future. An educated woman participates in the workforce, increases the gender diversity index of different sectors in society and provides new and different ideas and innovations. Increase in female labour participation will push the economic growth of the world. The International Labour Organization estimates that 865 million women in the world have the potential to contribute more fully to their economies. McKinsey Global estimates that $28 trillion could be added to the annual global GDP if women participated in the workforce at the same level as men.

The most important point is that any improvement in health leads to improvement in learning capabilities and skills and makes room for more working women, who will not just improve the life status of their families but contribute to the economy and their own financial freedom.

Monica Biradavolu is the CEO and Founder of QualAnalytics and is a Scholar-in-Residence at American University. She holds a PhD in Sociology from Duke University, and has held academic appointments at Yale, Duke and American University. She says, "Women are viewed, and view themselves, as caregivers, and not as care receivers. This does not mean that the women are the ones at fault. Norms of patriarchy condition everyone in society. Putting their needs last and every other family member's needs first remains the norm."

The thought of doing something for yourself first before doing it for your children will come across as selfish and self-serving and the antithesis of the idea of motherhood. "However, there must be a mental shift in thinking that taking care of oneself is the foundation upon which any caregiving role is built. Caring for yourself must go hand-in-hand with caring for others and these two are not either-or," she adds.

Healthy, educated, and preferably employed women are armed with awareness about a child's health, education, and overall development. But if mothers are unhealthy, they impact the rate of mortality and morbidity in infants and children too. According to studies, poor maternal health affects birth weight, neonatal survival, cognitive development, child behaviour, school performance, and adult health and productivity. It has also been proved that the ill health of children leaves long-term damage that affects the future generation. Studies have also found that if mothers die during childbirth, the children face increased mortality risk. The number of women and girls in India who died due to complications during pregnancy and childbirth in the year 2017 was as high as 35,000. Across India, there were 7,21,000 infant deaths in 2018, as per the United Nations' child mortality estimates. That's 1,975 infant deaths every day, on an average, in 2018, the highest in the world. National Family Health Survey-4 also reveals that the maternal mortality rate and under-five mortality rate of children decrease with the schooling of the mother and an increase in their financial status.

Hence, women's health has an intergenerational impact too. A healthy and educated mother ensures the forging of strong human capital that can participate in the labour force and contribute to global economic development.

The State of Women's Health

For a large part of our country, women are only considered functional because of their reproductive abilities and are often forced to bear children at the young age of 15–18. Early pregnancy is the major cause behind the rise of maternal deaths in India. At the age of 15 or 18, women's bodies are still developing and are not ready to bear the repercussions of pregnancy.

As a result, many women die due to pregnancy-related issues in their teenage years. Pregnancy-related complications are major reasons of death among 15–16 year-olds in India.

Navya Naveli Nanda, who runs a women's health product company, commented on how women have been conditioned to ignore their health. While discussing the core issues with me, she says, "Women don't necessarily prioritise their healthcare when it comes to family settings. It is always the health of the child, the health of the husband, and the health of the overall household that primarily come before the health of the women themselves. And I think this stems from the fact that women are so used to having their bodies controlled by everyone else but themselves."

And this issue is mainly because of the conditioning girls are put through at a very young age, by none other than the one person they trust the most—their mothers. Naveli adds, "I think from a very young age, we hear things like you are too skinny, you need to put on weight, how will you give birth in the future? Once you get married it is all about when are you having a child, when are you getting pregnant? It means more of a family event than something that stays between man and wife. That has almost led to this problem of women not being able to prioritise their own health and safety because they think it is something that is going to be controlled by someone else always."

Apart from pregnancy-related issues, women face more health risks compared to men. For example, heart disease is the leading cause of death among women in the United States. More women than men are diagnosed with mental health issues in a year. National Family Health Survey-5 has shown an increase in the rate of women (of age 15–49) being affected by anaemia. The rates of malnourished children and women have also seen an increase in the past few years. Lack of menstrual hygiene is reported to be the fifth biggest killer of women in the world after heart diseases, stroke, lower respiratory functions, and chronic illness. Eight lakh women die due to a lack of proper menstrual hygiene across the world in a year.

Nearly 3,00,000 women die due to pregnancy and childbirth across the world. A million others are adversely affected by illnesses that are avoidable or treatable. One in five women still get married early and many women are not using safe contraceptive methods to prevent childbirth. Sixty-eight thousand deaths happen annually due to unsafe abortions. HIV/AIDS affect women disproportionately more than men.

We need to understand why there is a lack of attention and awareness towards women's health. The primary reason which I have already talked about is male-child preference. The second reason is the idea of downplaying women's pain. Often, it is assumed that women complain overtly for small disruptions in their well being. Or that they are feigning their pain. Period pain, for example, is never taken seriously. Women who refuse to work or cry over period pain are often shut out as melodramatic. Women's pain is downplayed as negligible and not considered important enough to invest time, money, and effort on. This is despite the fact that women suffer from 70% of chronic pains and experience pain more acutely and intensely than men.

The major reason behind this bias is the patriarchal attitude that feeds on women's service and never considers their welfare important enough. The subservient nature of womanhood in a patriarchal society forces women to prioritise their health, choices and rights and uphold those of men. Moreover, the idea that women are internally weak also formulates the mindset that ignores women's pain as negligible.

Kamla's mother once visited a doctor in her area to seek treatment for over-sweating and panting. Her mother was disturbed by this problem for more than a week but she refused to visit a doctor because she was conditioned into believing that women's pain and health issues should not be prioritised. However, after a lot of convincing by her daughter, she finally visited a doctor. But she only received disappointment rather than proper treatment. The doctor dismissed her pain as psychological and refused to provide any medicines. Kamala's mother felt insulted and said that she will never visit a doctor again.

This is common in our society. Not only families but medical practitioners too play a role in dismissing women's pain and health issues. Kamala also once visited an eye surgeon in Varanasi to get a permanent solution of her myopia through lasik operation. She wears glasses of power as high as minus 10. But when she met the doctor, she was stunned by his response. He said that there is no need to conduct the surgery now but later when she is getting married. Kamala couldn't wrap her head around the fact that an educated professional dismissed her discomfort so casually. How could he suggest that removing eyeglasses should depend on a woman's marriage? Amidst the COVID-19 pandemic, visiting a doctor in Varanasi by travelling all the way from Bihar was a luxury but it shattered her expectation of fair treatment.

Disha Solanki and her mom were travelling from Delhi to Bangalore, a 36-hour arduous train journey through cities across the length of India. It is not easy to undergo such a long journey when you can't afford the luxury of a flight. "Although we were travelling in an AC coach, the greatest discomfort was to get access to a sanitised and safe loo. Although the government does its bit by providing washrooms in trains, it leaves the task undone by not ensuring their cleanliness and safety."

Disha says her mother, who suffers from an advanced level of OCD, refrained from using the washroom even once in the entire journey. "While I too had the cleanliness and sanitation issue, the bigger concern for me was the fear that someone might be lurking in or barge in to harass me."

This is not the first time that lack of access to a proper loo has bothered Disha and her mother. Even on their car rides to different cities and states, they find it very difficult to relieve themselves in public washrooms. They either don't go or ask somebody to accompany them to be safe. Moreover, there are not many public washrooms on highways and many women are forced to relieve themselves behind bushes which is dangerous considering the insects buzzing around and comes with the fear of being secretly watched by the passing cars on the highway. The problem is not the same for men. It is common for men to relieve themselves in open areas even though there are people watching. The reason is that the sight of men touching their genitalia and relieving themselves in public is not seen as scandalous and unsafe as it is for women.

It is unfortunate that women in our society do not have basic access to washrooms. Because of this, many women control themselves and wait until they reach a destination where they can relieve themselves without any worry. This affects their urinary glands, and ultimately their health.

Speaking about how holding up and not peeing affects women's health, Dr Sudeshna Ray says, "If women do not pee frequently, they create stagnant urine which is a seat for bacterial infection. So they are inviting urinary tract infections. Women also do not drink more water because they are scared that they will have to use the loo. Both these factors are sure shot factors for increasing the risk of UTI." She also adds, "If you do not pee for a long time, then your bladder muscles get overstretched. So, later on, women can have a lazy or overactive bladder and other urinary complications. In the case where there is no access to a clean loo, use any Indian toilet where physical contact is minimal, you are not coming in contact with anything, relieve yourself and then come home and clean it."

Furthermore, the medical and biological research that is conducted to understand the functions of the human body also reeks of gender biases. The male body is often considered the ideal human body and studies are based on this prejudice. As doctor Tanaya Narendra, physician, scientist, and embryologist, told women's platform *SheThePeople*, "There has been a long history of misogyny in medicine. Women's bodies were not understood well simply because male physicians were not allowed to examine or dissect female cadavers. Additionally, there was so much mystery around the idea of female genitals that no one really understood what they were and how they function."

Looking at this issue from a different perspective, Dr Kate Young, a public health researcher at Monash University in Australia, says, "Men have made the medical science about women and their bodies, and there is an abundance of research evidence about the ways in which that knowledge has been constructed to reinforce the hysteria discourse and women as reproductive bodies discourse. One of my favourite examples is that in some of the first sketches of skeletons, male anatomy artists intentionally made women's hips look wider and their craniums look much smaller as a way of saying: 'Here is our evidence that women are reproductive bodies and they need to stay at home and we can't risk making them infertile by making them too educated, look how tiny their heads are.' And we see that again and again." She further adds, "Any aspect of the female body that differs from the male or that cannot be given a male comparative (exemplified by the uterus) is viewed as evidence of deviation or 'fault'."

The focus on reproductive bodies has also meant that there is very little attention and awareness on women's post-reproductive health. There is abysmally little research on perimenopausal, menopausal, and postmenopausal changes in women's bodies.

Most doctors, researchers, and scientists have been men globally. In a global data of 2015, among 8,59,848 active physicians, 66% were men and only 34% women. Even today, many clinical trials do not involve women researchers and scientists. Research funding for male artery diseases is much more than women's even though they suffer from more morbidities. In 2005, eight of the ten prescriptive drugs were withdrawn from the US market because of their ill effects on women's health. This shows a lack of women in studies and trials of drugs and the waste of research funding due to the ignorance of women in clinical trials. Moreover, the human body or animal on which medical researches are performed are also male.

This brings me to the third reason why women's health is not taken seriously, which is the lack of medical facilities for women. Proper healthcare is a distant dream for many women in India. Women face gender biases in accessing healthcare facilities that are more readily available to men. The factors affecting the lack of healthcare facilities is the lack of transportation in rural areas, long-distance healthcare facilities, and the general idea that women's health is not the priority. This forces women to have patience and assume silence on pain and illness.

As a result, women are neither able to access basic preventive healthcare facilities nor prenatal or postnatal healthcare facilities. The medical practitioners themselves show a bias against women. These have been the central inspiration for me to drive conversations on *SheThePeople* and *Gytree*, the women's health platform. Women must have care, support, and judgement-free treatment from the start of their health journeys at 13 all the way to 55 years of age in terms of their hormonal health. And even beyond that for their immunity and bone strength and other chronic issues.

How can technology play a role? Monica Biradavolu says, "I think of tech as being critical in propagating the messages around self-care. Right now, this is restricted to select markets, largely urban and those who are financially better off." These messages need to become more widespread and I see tech as being an effective tool to reach more women.

"But two things need to happen—first, the concept itself needs to be better understood. Self-care includes regular health check-ups, but also includes things like having time in the day for yourself—maybe to exercise, maybe to relax, maybe to rest, more time off for working women—sick days, vacation days, and I think this is critical—not just advocating for women to speak up for themselves (which is very important) but also learning skills to negotiate with one's partner or other household members to get time for yourself without it becoming a dispute which leads to more tension and worse health."

Biradavolu has worked on a project with the UN Trust Fund for Women and learned from NGOs working in diverse settings that teaching both women and young girls about how to navigate familial relationships leads to more confidence, a greater feeling of control over one's life, and better emotional health.

"Second, in order to get the right tone, angle and make the message more 'indigenous' to women across geographies (urban, rural), languages, regions, social classes—the messaging needs to be carefully crafted. Needless to say, we must not forget to target men in these messages as well. To get it right, tech needs to work with partners—say, NGOs, marketing/ad agencies—to build tools that speak in a language that works in particular contexts."

Lakshmi Yalam lives in a village in Chhattisgarh. She was pregnant. As her delivery date was approaching, it was time to take her to the nearest hospital which was 15 km away. She also had to cross the Chintawagu river without any bridge. So how did the family manage? They carried Lakshmi in a utensil and crossed the river to reach the Bhopal Patnam Community Health Centre. Unfortunately, after all this effort, Lakshmi gave birth to a stillborn.

Devi Rani, a woman in Dehri-on-Sone of Bihar was married off as a child. After marriage, she was sent to live with her in-laws and husband in a different village. After a few months, she became pregnant even though her body was not ready to carry the burden of a foetus and childbirth. When it was time for her delivery, she was taken to a nearby government hospital. She was provided with no prenatal care which added to the complications in pregnancy that were present already because of her age. As a result, Devi died after giving birth to a child.

From their childhood, women aren't consuming enough nutrition or getting themselves preventive checks in an effort to put them on a path to holistic health. Families and doctors concentrate only on women's reproductive health in a way that's entirely divorced from their body's strength and make-up. This should draw our attention to the lack of awareness around the health of single and trans women. Health issues for single women are mostly ignored until it affects their reproductive health. Unmarried women in many families are never encouraged to go for regular medical check-ups. Women themselves internalise the deprioritisation of their health unless it affects their reproductive system. And as I have pointed out above, women are at more risk of morbidity due to cardiovascular diseases, heart attacks, and lung cancers.

Dr Sudeshna Ray says, "Women of reproductive age are not very prone to cardiovascular diseases or other diseases. Because they are protected with female hormones, menstrual hormones. But this is in case women have a regular cycle and balanced hormones. In case of women with hormonal imbalance, the risk increases. Moreover, when women reach menopause the risk of cardiovascular diseases becomes same as men. So the need for care also increases."

She also adds, "Just because women have hormonal balance, it doesn't mean families shouldn't be concerned about their health in general. Usually, families are concerned only about whether a woman is able to conceive on time or not. Families are mostly worried about pregnancy which is a small part of reproductive health. The whole thing comes from the idea that women must get married and have a child. There is a biological clock but there are other things also important in women's health."

Dharini Rampal, a single working woman in Navi Mumbai, was suffering from symptoms of depression for more than two years. But she kept ignoring them as unimportant and chided herself for malingering her suffering. But this only worsened her symptoms and at last she became suicidal and was diagnosed with the last stage of depression.

Trans women who are not reproducers and have a body that is different from the ideal human* body are often ignored as "faults" or unimportant in medical studies. There is a huge gap in data about the life expectancy of transgender people, the right dosages of medicines for their body, etc. There is a general lack of knowledge among doctors on how to address the health issues of transgender people. And because of this, there are high chances that transgender people are outright refused to be given proper treatment by doctors. But as reports suggest, transgender women carry the disproportionate burden of being infected by HIV. The percentage of clinical depression is also higher among transgender people. Transgender people often report having a lack of care providers, a lack of medical practitioners who have expertise in transgender medicine and can not only treat hormonal disbalance but general health issues too. Transgender bodies and issues are rarely taught about in conventional medical practice. Studies also show that there is a lack of effort to formulate the workforce needed for transgender healthcare or to determine the current status of transgender healthcare.

"Transgender body is a neglected area in terms of research. People did not come out with their transgender identity before. Now people are coming out with

*https://www.ncbi.nlm.nih.gov/pmc/articles/PMC5627669/

their transgender identity and are prone to different kinds of infections and different sort of imbalances in hormones. The research around transgender identity is evolving because more and more people are coming up with their transgender issues. However, more research needs to be done. The sociology and medical people need to concentrate on this area and make their health better," says Dr Ray.

Transgender activist, Trinetra Halder Gummaraj, notes that in MBBS, "Anal/oral sex, queer sexuality, perfectly healthy kink, gender non-conformity etc are grouped under sexual offences and sexual perversions." She also notes that in MBBS she was taught that homosexuality, transsexuality and transvestism are abnormal sexual behaviours. "To study absolute bogus in medical school with respect to my identity, and to vomit nonsense in exams for marks was absolutely traumatising. Imagine your classmates learning that you are some freak of nature from qualified doctors. I was suicidal," Gummaraj says.

As pointed out earlier too there is a lack of research on women's bodies and health problems. This adds to the lack of approachability of basic healthcare for women. Many women are not able to access basic healthcare facilities, others who can access do not get adequate treatment. Information on women's health issues is not something that women are taught about from an early age. We live in a society where periods, vagina and related health problems are hush topics. Neither mothers nor fathers educate their daughters about menstruation, reproduction, breast cancer, PCOD, and other health problems. Rather than education about women's health, the silence around accessing or prioritising health is normalised in our society.

It is not a hidden fact that even today, women feel shy to talk about their health problems related to their reproductive organs. And now, because they don't express their concerns, they do not receive proper care.

The general ignorance towards women's health concerns and the taboo related to their bodies further affects the knowledge of women about their bodies. So many women do not discuss their health problems with men in the house who have control over the decisions taken at home.

In India, breast cancer accounts for 14% of cancers in Indian women. It is reported that every four minutes, an Indian woman is diagnosed with breast* cancer.

In a survey in America** of 9,000 women, only 9.4% were aware of the risk of breast cancer. Four in 10 women never discussed the risk of breast cancer with their doctors. Forty-six per cent, which mainly included white women, were likely to overestimate the risk of breast cancer while 45% which included Black, Asian, and Hispanic women, underestimated it. In a recent survey conducted on 2,800 women in India, 65% of women are unaware of polycystic ovary syndrome (PCOS) symptoms (which include having infrequent or prolonged menstrual periods or excess male hormone)

---

*https://timesofindia.indiatimes.com/blogs/poverty-of-ambition/breast-cancer-in-india/

**http://webmd.com/women/news/20130904/most-women-dont-understand-their-breast-cancer-risk-survey while 25% are not aware of it at all even though one out of every five women in India suffers from it.

"Even the remotest of villages have access to beauty care. If you ask most women, they have certain ideas about beauty care but not health because that is not important to them. Or at least they do not think health issues are important to them. Most of the women are very inhibited when talking about their health. They just don't talk about their problems with the elders or husbands and just suppress. So there is more ignorance than unawareness about diseases among women."

Dr Ray adds, "Of course, there is a lack of information among women about certain diseases but today the internet has reached the interiors of India. There is also a lack of access to a properly trained doctor. I go for a camp where people have to travel for six miles to come to a hospital. For them it is like one day of no earning and food if they have to see a doctor."

Even if some women try to gather information about their health, the lack of research around women's bodies and silence around their sexuality that seeps in the hospitals too makes it difficult for women to know about their bodies. As pointed above, the male body has always been seen as the ideal body for medical research. So many doctors do not know about women's issues or how certain health problems affect women differently from men.

For years, the National Institute of Health based in the US wasn't keeping a track of female enrollment in medical research. Women of childbearing age were prohibited from being a part of the drug trials.

Researchers were reluctant to include women in medical research for two reasons. First was the paternalistic reason of the research possibly affecting women's reproductive system. And the second was general laziness, because hormonal changes in women made the data more complicated. This gender bias in medical research, which is slowly changing but not effectively, has skewed the knowledge about women's health. For example, many medical practitioners are still unaware that women in their 80s don't usually face chest and left arm pain during heart attacks. They face other symptoms like fatigue, nausea, and jaw and neck pain. So a woman's pain and symptoms often seem atypical for the research that has been conducted on male subjects.

As a result, women have to be dependent on their family's knowledge about women's health. And if women are caught up in patriarchal families, the awareness and importance of women's health is further ignored.

How Other Countries Are Improving the Status of Women's Health

Lack of awareness and infrastructure for women's health is a predicament faced by most developing nations, the major issues being high maternal mortality rate, female genital cutting, cervical cancer and more. But many countries have begun focusing on improving the status of women's health and hence contributing to the growth of the economy. The US, for instance, has been focusing on international family planning activities, maternal and child health, nutrition, and reproductive health programmes.

The World Health Organization and United Nations Volunteers programme launched an initiative named African Women Health Champions. This programme recruited 100 women from Africa to support WHO in improving the health of people in African countries and also promote gender equality.

The Minister of Health in Australia launched the National Women's Health Strategy 2020–2030 to focus on women's health which identifies policy gaps and new and emerging health issues for women and girls.

South Asian countries, on the other hand, have improved both maternal mortality and child mortality rates by training more female healthcare workers and providing affordable care for mothers and children. But the journey has been slow and needs more concerted efforts across government departments and large-scale campaigns. We also need to tailor needs and focus on women who don't want to have children, stay single, and make other identity and gender choices.

Women and Mental Health

The major causes of the higher prevalence of mental health disorders among women are sexual violence, the burden of unpaid domestic work, and other patriarchal oppressions that force women to conform to set ideals. Despite the higher prevalence of mental disorders, women's mental health is not valued. Even if a woman tries to be expressive about her mental health, her issues are shunned by the stereotype that women have no workload and the consequent stress. Mostly, mental health disorders among women are grouped as malingering or signs of weakness.

Rajshri, who lives in Patna, Bihar, and is a writer, has been suffering from acute depression for the last few years. It began with the strained environment at home, as the first symptoms of depression occurred when she was in 10th grade. But the depression spiralled downward after a major incident in her life. Rajshri was harassed by her hostel superintendent.

While she was removed from the hostel, her parents kept quiet about the harassment incident and encouraged her to forget or ignore it. This worsened her mental health and then the pandemic hit, breaking down any scope of her finding an external outlet for change or help. Her depression turned into suicidal tendencies and she continues to struggle with good and bad weeks. Rajshri's case is not one-off. Thousands of girls, abused by strangers or family, have for years suffered in silence. Many have taken their lives and others lived with no recourse for help. These girls usually grow up and ask their own daughters to hide such incidents.

The national crime report of 2018 showed that housewives were the second largest group who died by suicide because of being harassed by their husbands and in-laws through dowry harassment and domestic violence.

Author Vandana Kohli, who writes on the issue, puts it in perspective. "It makes women feel entrapped. Anybody who feels they are being watched over all the time will come under tremendous strain." She also says,

"When a woman is shaken in her emotional sense of wellness, then it directly impacts the family, especially the children. Because women are the loci of the family system. Therefore, for not just women alone, but for the sake of family and society, women's mental health and emotional wellbeing should be valued."

Therapist Rhea Raghav Dubey, who works with many young children and girls says that once a woman gets married she loses her identity. "Then how can a woman without an identity raise a child with an identity?"

Talking specifically about married women, Dubey adds that if there is no emotional or physical intimacy among partners in a relationship, it leads to dissociation with the sense of self which ultimately affects the mental health of women. So it is important to talk about men and their freedom to be expressive when we talk about the mental health of women.

"The issue is not just about the lack of language around the mental health of women but also the lack of women psychologists and psychiatrists," says Rajshri who rejected many doctors because they thought she was "going through a phase".

"It is not common for women to express their issues in front of anyone because they are conditioned to not speak up about their emotions and feelings. Having female psychologists is crucial to providing a comfortable space for women to express their issues because women psychologists have higher chances to understand and empathise with women patients."

Rajshri herself felt the difference in meeting a female psychologist and a male psychiatrist. While meeting the male psychiatrist, she could only talk about the physical symptoms she was facing. But when she met a female therapist and psychologist, she could find a comfortable space to talk about traumas and thoughts. The female psychologist too was understanding enough to listen to Rajshri and to not reveal her past to her parents.

But, as Kohli points out, there is an impasse among women too when it comes to discussing mental health issues. She says that the first reason is pride. Some women feel that if they speak about their mental health issues with someone then somehow their pride will be affected or they will be judged and taken advantage of. The second reason is loyalty. If women have a problem with one person in the family and want to talk about it, they will put her husband and his entire family in a bad light. The third is the fear that women have of losing financial independence, resources and support if they speak up about their issues with someone else.

So, what's needed is many efforts across society and its temperament along with facilities that enable women to find an outlet and solution to their needs for mental health.

A sisterhood is another way of finding answers. When I envisioned *Gytree* as a women's health platform, I realised how many of us are shy of talking about our health challenges and journeys. As a result, *Gytree*—other than offering all women's health products and services in one place—has created communities led by women who have lived experiences of specific diseases and is able to openly share the same with other women, in a private and judgement-free manner.

When women are empowered and come together to support each other, it can work wonders in improving health-seeking behaviours.

This was shown impressively by an initiative called Avahan to combat HIV/AIDS in India. Avahan worked with one of the most highly stigmatised and marginalised groups of women globally, not just in India—sex workers. Saroja is a sex worker who lives in Rajahmundry, Andhra Pradesh. Her husband drank his life away. Penniless and struggling to feed her three children, she was introduced to sex work by a woman in her neighbourhood. She started doing sex work by soliciting and entertaining clients, mostly long-distance truckers, who knew where to find her—sitting in the mango and guava orchards that line the national highway that cuts through Rajahmundry. At first she was unsure and scared, but over time she became used to the work. For one thing, it made economic sense. If she worked hard as a day labourer in the agricultural fields or at construction sites, she would make ₹150–200 at the end of a long gruelling day of backbreaking work in the sun. For a 5 or 10-minute "encounter" with a client in the mango orchard, she earned ₹50. Besides, she was sometimes asked for sexual favours for "free" by overseers. Why not get paid for it? An added benefit was that she was the mistress of her own time and her "worksite" was in the shade. But there were dangerous downsides—she was terrified of her secret being discovered by her family, there were significant health risks of STIs and HIV and there was the ever-present threat of violence, and sometimes actual violence, by clients and the police. That changed when Avahan came into the picture.

When women are empowered and come together to [illegible] each other, [illegible] confidence in [illegible] health-seeking behaviour.

This was shown impressively by an NGO [illegible] to combat HIV/AIDS in Nepal. [illegible] worked with [illegible] and the most highly stigmatised and marginalised group of women [illegible] sex worker who lives in Kathmandu [illegible]. Her husband died [illegible] to feed her [illegible] was introduced [illegible] by a woman [illegible] started doing sex work [illegible] and [illegible] mostly [illegible] highway that runs around Kathmandu. At first, she was [illegible] and scared but over time she [illegible] used to the work. For one thing, it made economic sense. If she worked hard [illegible] she would make [illegible] 250 [illegible] the end of a long [illegible] day [illegible] in the [illegible] 5 or 10 [illegible]

[illegible] health [illegible] risk of STIs and HIV and there was [illegible] of violence and [illegible] in [illegible] and the police [illegible] when [illegible]

In India, over 59% of the female workforce drops out because of health issues. Every four minutes a woman is diagnosed with breast cancer. India is 55th on the Hologic World Women's Health Index among 116 countries.

The good news is that many solutions will come from technology.

We need to foster a culture of learning about our bodies, understanding how they function, prevent basic problems simply by following a primary healthcare routine, and not land up at the doctor's when it's too complex or too late.

With the pandemic, women are more open to using telemedicine and get a diagnosis online. Imagine this—a space that is targeted at women's health, helps them focus on specific issues from anemia to vaginal discharge, and offers them a safe environment to have doctor-patient conversations. This is so important and I am on a mission to build this. Young women are going to seek changes, and transform what healthcare looks like because while make-up may be good to do, health for them will become must-do.

So, where are we today?

We are facing a big knowledge gap on what women need to know about their bodies, have agency over it, and adopt ways to live longer and stronger lives. It's high time we see the female body for what it truly is—a complex system that goes through many different stages from 15 to 55. Undoubtedly, we need a razor-sharp focus on how each cycle should be approached—from prevention to treatment.

"Femtech" is the new frontier, creating change and

impacting the lives of women positively by offering specific care for their needs. While this is rapidly growing around South East Asia and America, we need to see more significant investments in platforms creating the winning combination of services and products.

Our goal for India's 700 million women should be to make themselves a priority and help them understand what steps they can take to improve their health.

India's history has so many female doctors who fought the system to shine and made medicine a relevant and respectable profession for women. From India's first woman doctor, Anandibai Joshi, who went to America to fulfil the absence of female physicians across India to Kadambhini Ganguly, who became India's first practicing doctor while also raising eight children. Each year, thousands of students become doctors because this is a great career for women, they are told. Ironically, most Indian women don't see access to health as a priority.

At home during lockdowns, women picked up the lion's share of unpaid care responsibilities, from childcare to looking after the sick and the elderly. Vital health and support services targeting women and girls have been severely disrupted, while reports of domestic violence have increased.

Women and girls have specific and diverse health needs which must be met now, and they have equal rights to participate in, and benefit from, global recovery efforts in a post-pandemic world.

empower the status of women in society by offering opportunities for them [illegible] growing and in South East Asian countries, women are the most significant part in the labour, earning for women's contribution of services and produce.

Our goal for India's 500 million women is to make certain that it is reaching a great deal of quality and vital capacity we can to improve their health.

India's nation has so many female doctors who [illegible] from India's first woman doctor, [illegible] physicians [illegible] who became India's first [illegible] might consider [illegible] students become doctors because this is a great career for women that [illegible] to health as a person.

[illegible] India's women [illegible] the world's [illegible] unpaid [illegible] workers, from childcare to looking after the sick and the elderly. Vital health and support services targeting women and girls have been severely disrupted, while reports of domestic violence have risen.

Women and girls have specific and diverse health needs which must be met now, and they have equal rights to participation and benefit in global recovery efforts in a post-pandemic world.

lower socioeconomic and educational backgrounds. But at the same time, this industry is nearly entirely unorganised. The founder of a startup, which offers on-demand beauty services via its app, claims only 5% of this market is organised. This is because most people avail local services in their neighbourhood, or call a parlour didi who is familiar to them.

It was this sort of parlour didi loyalty that led 45-year-old Sandhya Sharma, mother of two sons, to set up her own little salon in Dehri-on-Sone, in Rohtas district of Bihar. Sandhya was brought up in Uttar Pradesh where her father worked in a small factory. Growing up seeing the women in the house always being so submissive, at the young age of five, Sandhya realised the person with money in their hands had the power. And so she made that her goal—to become independent and earn when she grew up. Sandhya was married at 11, soon as she got her first period, shattering all her dreams.

She was burdened with marriage and other responsibilities that came with it at a young age, marrying a man of 22, twice her age. “My in-laws realised I was too young and deserved to do something with myself. I asked to do a beautician’s course.” But doing the course wasn’t enough inspiration for her to start working. Her husband would beat her each time he returned home after drinking and that became Sandhya’s real trigger to take the plunge and set up a tiny little parlour.

Domestic abuse is one of the many reasons why women leave home for work. But there is one more reason. Women are forced to get out and work because their husbands are either incompetent, out drinking, or just too used to eating off others rather than working themselves. "Sometimes having your own space is about having a safe area to chit chat, laugh out loudly and have some friends," says Sandhya.

Anita Rautela works as a masseur in a building in Gurgaon, the urban suburb outside of Delhi populated with a large number of working professionals. A mother to four (the youngest is a boy as her husband wouldn't stop till she produced one), she used to work as a cook and then realised that that wasn't adding up to enough. So she started taking up beauty and massage services. At ₹400 a massage she earns, in a regular month, close to ₹40,000 for the family. Her husband, an auto rickshaw driver, heads to work only on days he isn't too lazy to wake up. "I have to earn to ensure our children are raised. What's worse is that I have three daughters and my husband wouldn't stop until a boy was born." That leaves Anita no choice but to work—both outside and at home. "But there is one advantage of stepping out, I get to meet women who are empowered and that is such a big inspiration for me to keep going. Aaj kal ki didis, kaam karti hain and mujhe himmat deti hai."

None of these women have bank accounts and nor are they part of the employment pool that feeds into the numbers in India's economy. In fact, to most people, it appears these women are not even employed. But these women are running their homes, getting themselves some dignity, and becoming financially capable.

In India, 95% or around 195 million women are employed in the unorganised sector or in unpaid labour, says a report released by consultancy firm Deloitte. This sector defines activities not covered by

Predicaments of Women Involved in Informal Sectors

There's another fascinating aspect of beauty parlour economics in little towns. It's a wonderful source of "lift me up" when women don't have a place to go and talk about their personal, professional, economic, or emotional challenges. They make friends, they create a sisterhood and this, in turn, produces new opportunities. One such opportunity is economic.

A kitty, community, or a beesi are different words for an informal set up where women contribute small amounts to get a lump sum at the end of a certain time cycle. These are prevalent across income groups in India but the impact of having access to community funds in especially low-income and informal sectors has a material impact on their lives and urgent needs. These contributory groups are based on trust between members of a community, who are empathetic to one of their own whose husband needs medical care or whose child's school fees must be paid.

India is home to 90%* of the informal labour force and has the world's largest informal economy. And within the informal economy, women have the largest share of labour.

Studies show that women working in the informal sector receive less than half the wage that men involved in the same sector receive. There is also a gender stereotype that dictates and divides the labour between

*https://www.indiaspend.com/uploads/2021/03/26/file_upload-446784.pdf

men and women. For example, men and women working in the domestic care sector have different salaries and responsibilities based on their gender. A woman is subjected to "feminine" work like cooking and cleaning with less salary, while men take up jobs as drivers and gardeners which entitle them to comparatively more salaries. The women-dominated sectors of the informal economy, like beauty parlours, pay less than the male-dominated sectors like construction sites.

The reason why many women choose to or are forced to work in the informal sector is that they need a job that can help them balance both their familial responsibilities and work. Ruby says that she may not have opted for a full-time job in the organised salon market because she wants flexibility but adds quickly that she is nonetheless contributing to the economy. How is that, I ask her.

"My service helps working women to get rid of the week's tiredness in one day. I offer flexibility to the client and I am able to do the service for a far more reasonable rate than a big parlour." An average Indian woman spends around ₹3,000–4,000 a year on beauty salons. This market at all levels—organised or informal—is growing at 15% a year. With the COVID-19 pandemic, people have increased at-home services to avoid public area contact. Women are the central workforce for this sector. Could there be a better way to measure their contribution as self-employed even though their earnings don't make it to the financial system?

During COVID-19, it was expected that gig jobs would allow women who have domestic and care

Ruby Devi and Sandhya Sharma, women working in the informal sector, are burdened with the lack of capital and time to handle housework and work together. Women are brought up with the psychology that they should be satisfied with what is available to them, rather than aiming higher.

But if work done by women in the informal sector is respected as much as those under the organised sector, they will be encouraged to dream of more. Their responsibilities at home and at work should be recognised as valid sectors of employment. They should be provided with enough credit and security so that they can collect the capital to expand their business.

Chetna Gala Sinha of the Mann Deshi Mahila Sahakari Bank has been working with women for years and helping them get small loans without hesitation. Sinha began organising women for smaller projects such as demanding toilets or electricity. "My house had become somewhat of a centre where women would come to vent. Yet, not a single person ever asked for money directly—that's not how they think. They simply want opportunity," she says in an interview with *Outlook*[*] magazine. "Women would borrow from the pool to buy goats and buffaloes mainly, and would pay it back through weekly instalments, and unfalteringly so, lest they be ousted from this support system."

"Women are much more vulnerable to a range of lifecycle risks than men," says Parul Seth Khanna whose platform Pinbox works with women and offers them microloans. "They earn lower incomes than

---

*https://wow.outlookbusiness.com/chetna-gala-sinha/

men, are disproportionately more self-employed, face frequent work interruptions, make up the majority of single-earner households, and are also more financially excluded."

"On the other hand, women are much more careful about their money, more focused on risk management, and work harder to improve the lives of their children and families. Women are also much more disciplined than men when it comes to both savings and repaying loans. It's not surprising therefore that nearly 90% of the 40 million micro-credit customers in India are women. But the number of self-employed women is growing rapidly. And many more women urgently need easier and more reasonable institutional access to formal credit for livelihoods—for setting up or expanding their micro-enterprises."

The point is, women need to be encouraged to step into the entrepreneurial world, even if they start small. As per *Powering The Economy With Her: Women Entrepreneurship In India*, published jointly by Google and Bain & Company, women business owners can create around 150 million to 170 million jobs in India by 2030. Since small and medium enterprises are the second-largest employers in India after agriculture and contribute to over 30% of GDP, it is imperative to encourage women to build small businesses.

The beauty parlour is symptomatic of many such sectors where women can find more than just employment.

"I stunned a man by telling him I would orgasm first. It's almost like he was disinterested in the plan right after that."

Most women said they were constantly made to believe they had no sexual entitlement, just as much as they are made to think women deserve lesser pay, demotion due to pregnancies, and other glass ceilings. The fact that they couldn't rightly claim pleasure in their lives just like anything else seemed like such an internalised crisis.

Could this have a lot to do with the fact that women are mainly considered walking wombs or baby bearers and quite nothing beyond that? One wonders where all of this self-doubt, self-sacrifice comes from.

History's problematic lexicon is the reason for the many obscure ways in which women are treated even today. The word "hysterical" for example comes from the Latin "hystericus" ("of the womb"). Apparently, in the 19th century, there was a trend of surgeons removing healthy ovaries to treat "ailments" such as hysteria.

Rachel Gross writes in *The Guardian*, "In ancient Greece, women were believed to be controlled by their unruly wombs—with the unruliness often caused by a failure to bear children in a timely manner. If she stayed unmarried too long after puberty, it was thought, a woman's uterus would trample around her body like a bratty toddler, causing all manner of unpleasant symptoms. That idea would ultimately evolve into the notion of hysteria, with its roots in the Greek word for womb, hustera. The removal of the uterus is still called a hysterectomy. Suddenly it all appears so inappropriate and wrong because it outrightly shames women for no fault of theirs.

These conversations became my inspiration behind starting a new show called *Sisterhood on YouTube*, to elevate ourselves from self-imposed shame, doubts about things, and have a platform for women (and some men) to have these discussions fearlessly. We started talking about issues that not only remain a taboo, but also spark a polar view in the society. For example, female pleasure was the subject we explored for the debut episode and asked why women only wanted to claim their space on the streets and not in the sheets. Part of the issue was what we grew up knowing about sex. As actor Swara Bhaskar says on the show, "I used to think if you stay in a room at night with a boy you become a bin beyahee maa (mother out of wedlock)."

While we navigate confusing and often conflicting messages about our bodies, misconceptions about sexuality, and a lack of information when it comes to queer experiences—we are actually having sex, and lots of it. This isn't just in urban centres, but also in villages and in cities, off dating apps and in WhatsApp sexts, with partners, husbands, friends, ex-es, and friendly strangers. Even with ourselves. But still the orgasm gap persists, so does shame and scandal around us having sex and actually enjoying it. And this has dangerous, lethal consequences. Rape culture thrives, sex continues to be used as a weapon against women and other genders, and their bodies continue to be policed. Pop culture has a big role to play here as well. Trinetra Haldar talks of where we have gone wrong in portraying trans women as people who must claim

in the relationship and a lower divorce rate. While there is no detailed research yet on women and a correlation with their sexual satisfaction, our platform *SheThePeople* did ask women if feeling sexually happy and content helped them become better at work.

"It's so difficult to measure something that's so sublime. But if I had a sexually dissatisfied life, I would definitely show some frustration at work, at friends, or life. We all need good endorphins to function. A good sex life is that too for women," Ruhi Das says, in a rather practical tone.

A happy sex life is an important part of a fulfilling life notes an article by a health app. What a happy sex life means is subjective, as our sexual desires, expectations* and needs differ from one another and change as we grow and age. Some people want to have sex daily, while other people are content with a lot less. The article adds, a person's partner has a strong influence on their sexual experience. In a study of Iranian women, more than 7 out of 10 women with sexual dysfunction reported that the cause of their dysfunction was related to interpersonal problems with their partner.

Das adds, women are never encouraged to have agency over their sexual lives. "Even though Indian women are having sex, and a lot of it, it's not clear whether they are experiencing pleasure or asking for their rightful place in the bed."

A 2019 sex survey across India showed the average age at which Indians have their first sexual encounter

*https://helloclue.com/articles/sex/science-sexual-satisfaction

has fallen significantly. In 2003, only 8% of respondents said their first sexual encounter took place before the age of 18. In 2019, almost a third of respondents said their first encounter took place in their teens, according to the survey conducted by *India Today* magazine.

The survey argues that more the things have changed in the Indian sexual arena, the more they have also remained the same. In their larger sexual attitudes, men remain trapped in the past, as the results of their survey showed. To the question—"Is virginity important to you?"—53% of respondents (both men and women) said yes.

"Something like this will not just create misconceptions, it will deter girls from having a conversation with friends, mothers, and will cement the idea of virginity as a big deal when its just not needed," says Manasi Shah, who lives in Rajkot and has had many arguments with her family about her open sexual life since she gave up hiding it.

Shah's mother was petrified about her daughter getting pregnant. "On the one hand, they don't want to discuss sex and contraception and on the other they will find the most bizarre reasons to claim that going out with men or other partners is going to land up in pregnancy."

This, when Indian women, in the past decade, especially in urban India, have come into their own, gained some financial independence, made strides professionally, and taken patriarchy and misogyny head-on. A wave of feminism that has also bred a liberal attitude towards sex. But even as most women are no longer afraid to seek pleasure as equals, they are also scared of being judged.

One day she finally asked him point blank. He said he could not think of having sex with her, she who gave birth to his children. She was stumped. Since then, they have taken recourse to online counselling. Surprisingly, her husband cooperated, and they are working on their sex life.

This is but one such reason for a sexless marriage and fortunately the couple realised it very early in their marriage. There have been cases where couples go without having sex for as much as six months to two to three years or more. A survey had found that only 20% of Indian couples had sex more than once a week, down from 37% a decade ago. Well, you might ask if many Indians are in a sexless marriage, how come the country is counted among the most populous in the world?

Having sex for pleasure and procreation are two different things. You might come across many people, especially women, who think having sex is just a necessity for having babies. That's one of the many reasons behind sexless marriages in India.

Many women I spoke to admitted to living two separate lives. One, where they toe the line, live by family rules, don't talk about themselves or their personal and sexual needs, and then there is a life they have on the internet hidden behind avatars and personas. One wonders why they need to live in these compartments. "We are conditioned and we don't know how to communicate about our pleasure and desires with our partners. Worse, our partners are not conditioned to hear it from us. In any case, honestly, the men are all the time swiping on dating sites and watching the internet for sexual content. It's only because women are now talking about themselves doing this, we are suddenly having to answer questions." Rohini Rajagopal, who lives outside of Pune near Lonavala, makes a good point.

"A woman who knows what she wants, and claims right to her sexual wellbeing is called a slut," says 18-year-old Ariana Singh who just passed out of a school in Gurgaon. Why should shame always be the inheritance of women? She asks. "Some urban young girls like me are torn between having progressive parents or moms who will keep us aware of our world but we end up stating our point of view, and look at how friends, family and others just glare at our guts to 'want' or to 'desire'."

Another reason why sexual pleasure is such a taboo discussion is because many women have direct or indirect experience of sexual trauma and that has left them terrified of wanting sexual rights and they end up considering the idea of sexual emancipation as something that's dirty and inappropriately sexualised. "Ask a girl in India if she has been molested as a child, young adult or adult and the answer is in her look—duh, of course, that guy who pinched me in the bus, the auto driver who shagged in front of me, or that uncle who held my buttocks or that cousin who discovered his sexuality by experimenting on my ignorance," Anubavi Sharma, quips with a sense of the obvious. "All of us have been through something horrific, hidden from our families, because 'Haawwwww, how can you accuse your cousin?'"

And so, for Indian women, learning about sexual

[illegible] informed [illegible] quick women [illegible] techniques [illegible] than [illegible] a good man.

A woman who knows what she wants and clearly [illegible] partner [illegible] have [illegible] [illegible] [illegible] pleasure [illegible]

Another reason [illegible] pleasure is [illegible] because many women have [illegible] and the comforting the idea of sexual [illegible] something [illegible]. Ask a girl in India if she has been molested as a child [illegible] or adult and the answer [illegible] that girl who touched me in the bus, that [illegible] who held my [illegible] or that cousin who discovered his sexuality by experimenting on me [illegible]

[illegible] to have been [illegible] something [illegible] hidden [illegible] of our [illegible] because [illegible] how can you [illegible]

And for the Indian woman, talking about sexual

who enjoys a mutually respectful sexual relationship with her partner comes out as a more confident and happier person and is able to take a call for herself. Whereas sexually dissatisfied women walk in with a low confidence, unhappiness and look generally disturbed and inattentive," Sudeshna adds.

Rowland also adds why equality in sheets goes a long way in helping women claim their power. "It's far harder to rewire biology than it is to alter belief. While their paths to sexual healing varied, the women I spoke to made plain that satisfaction was rooted in their social power, in being entitled to explore and express their sexuality and in feeling equal to their partners. Pleasure and its value can be learned, and once learned, are not readily relinquished."

To me, as an author, it was clear that sexual agency and rights to pleasure are integrally linked with how women unleash themselves and build confidence. Since we have not adequately paid attention to women's right to pleasure, we have simply ignored this and let women underestimate their sexuality and sexual needs. And this must change.

chapter ten

Single and Rocking It

"I have never seen marriage as a necessity, it's more for society," says Kishi Arora, who works as a pastry chef in New Delhi. "You can live with someone for companionship and live with them and love them and you don't need to conform. I never saw this as a compulsion." Arora is a pastry chef, who recently lost her dad, and now lives in a two-storey home where her mom stays below and she occupies the other floor. As a chef she is busy organising the day's orders in her professional at-home kitchen with a hydroponic vegetable garden.

Kishi has no intentions of getting married and would rather spend her life being a caregiver to her mom and pursuing her own interests. And that just somehow becomes the most intriguing part of every conversation she has. "How can you not want to get married? Your clock is ticking." On this count her parents were not different though they did come around eventually. "They did of course want me to get married. I am the oldest of three children. They wanted me to have a 'normal' life like all their friends' daughters had."

For Indian girls, what's normal is that marriage is a goal. Sometimes the only goal. They are fed on a diet of Bollywood films that promises them a life of "happily ever after" or believe their good fortune will turn like a page of Jane Austen's many novels, where women validate their social standing and economic status by finding a rich young man to marry.

Increasingly though, as Indian society opens up, many women are realising this fallacy that it isn't worth the future and that finding a Mr Right needn't be the aim of every woman. In fact, many believe that single women can lead wholeheartedly happy, solitary, and fulfilling lives.

India has 72 million single women. That's bigger than the populations of UK and Switzerland put together. This includes widows, divorcees, unmarried women, and women who are separated from their husbands. Of this figure, 13 million single mothers are heading households, which is a telling statistic by itself.

There are historic reasons why women like Kishi want to break free and why many aren't able to. In society and on screen. We have normalised women as people who lay the table, do the laundry, cook delicious meals, "keep the family together", sacrifice the last roti, never talk of their education or achievements, lower their voice, "conform" to patriarchy and are often the eye/arm candy for the man.

We have never seen or celebrated single women on television, in films, in novels and comics. It's as if she didn't exist except for that occasional widowed bua who always sat in the kitchen and looked out of the window in a white sari (in India widows are expected to wear only white clothes after her husband dies as a sign of austerity, though this is changing in the metropolitan cities). In society too, the single woman is looked down upon in many gatherings, as though she was the home wrecker, the husband-snatcher, or undeserving to be out and about, enjoying her life by herself.

Society's Prescription for Marriage

The way we think of marriage is a big reason why lives of single women receive no attention in Indian society. Wife, husband, and kids. This is how we have been conditioned to imagine a traditional and happy family. Anything that deviates from this assumption is sidelined as a fault line or damage and blamed on the woman. Marriage in Indian society is not understood in terms of companionship but in terms of financial and social security for women and the onus of "success" in a marriage hinges on her.

This is the reason that while 95% of marriages in India are arranged (that is to say, the couple doesn't find each other and fall in love but it's the families that fetch the partner), we only have a divorce rate of less than 1%. In comparison, Luxembourg has the highest rate of divorces at 87%, and the US records 46%.

So out of 1,000, only 13 marriages end in divorce in India as per a BBC report. Does this mean Indians are rocking married lives? Absolutely not. A combination of patriarchal values, "sanctity" of marriages in Indian society, religious beliefs, and the lack of women's participation in the workforce and therefore the inability to earn for themselves are among the many reasons why Indian women suffer abusive, loveless, sexless marriages.

As a result, singlehood is not seen as a norm for women. Neena Gupta, one of India's iconic actors made headlines for decades for being a woman who chose to have a baby out of wedlock with her boyfriend, legendary cricketer, Viv Richards. Their daughter Masaba Gupta is now a young fashion designer and a breakthrough actor. "I speak to so many liberated women and men, who are well travelled and have experienced marriage or painful marriages, everyone believes it's the most natural progression in a woman's life. I understand marriage as an idea for companionship but not something just to have a baby," she says in an interview with *SheThePeople*. A single or divorced woman still manages to raise eyebrows that question her character, her legitimacy as a good and respectable woman, and her ability to live her life on her own. One must ask why we don't raise such objections when it comes to single or divorced men or why single men are seen in terms of opportunity or sympathy while single women are criticised as immoral, imperfect, or inauspicious?

While morality is the society's favourite stick, women are often made to feel guilty of seeking more from their lives.

"How can a mother do this to her children?" Sarita Moga was asked when she tried to leave her drunk wife-beater husband. Rohini Srinivas was ridiculed for seeking higher education because she was becoming "overqualified" compared to her husband. When she wanted to work, a village meeting was held on how "inappropriate" it was for a girl to have "such" dreams.

The Idea of "Settling" Down

"Settle down" is what society asks a woman to do when she has finished her minimum education and has attained the standard marriageable age (in some parts of India that can be as low as 16 or 18).

When India's top-ranked tennis player, who has won six grand slam titles, was interviewed, a journalist asked her, "When are you planning to settle down?" Sania Mirza countered him by asking, "You don't think I am settled?"

At the time, she had already gained financial success and glory in her career, yet she was asked this question. Sania is now married with a child but this "settle down" piece takes a new meaning for women who don't really want to opt for settling down.

Women like Kishi are not ready to conform to the traditions and want to build their own lives and careers. And I cannot see a fault in that. Why should marriage be the only way in which a woman can attain happiness, love, and security? Why can't women choose to be the decision-makers and bread earners of their own lives rather than depending on a man or marriage for the same?

"I am not ready to settle down with something," Kishi Arora voices her choices and paves a new way for the freedom of many other women who find the idea of "settling down" in having a solid career, being with parents, living alone, and pursuing passions.

"When my dad was sick, he was scared that when he was gone, I would be alone with my mom. And what will happen to me," Kishi remembers. "There has not been a time when my friends came and my dad didn't complain to them. My dad would give me resumes of boys at all times. I wasn't here to hire someone. You will be with a guy, he will let you live on your own terms, is what he said. But I was never open to the idea of arranged marriage. I can't do this."

These are ways young people are slowly changing the perceptions. They are making choices and are content with those choices. With millions of single women around the country, what's absent is a real conversation in the media about the role these women are playing and can play in economic progress.

Our Understanding of Marriage

We mainly understand marriage by witnessing the relationship, dynamics, and roles between our parents and relatives. If we have grown up witnessing unequal, unhappy, and abusive marriages, happy marriage might rarely seem a possibility. As grown-ups, we either internalise marriages to be an unhappy relationship or dare to question it. Kishi chose the second option. She came from a small-town family, but in school she met people from different walks of life, different kinds of parents. Her friends had parents who were fighting, some had parents who were rich and mostly absent.

"In my house, the deal was mom makes the meals, dad comes in the evening, and we had a lot of time together, warmth, and love. My mom would make hot chapatis. My friends, some cousins, too, behaved like they lived in a hotel," says Kishi.

"I think we all experience trauma in different ways within our families. What is normal for me, isn't normal at all for others."

"I saw marriage through my aunts. We were from a small town. Man works outside. Women work with chores and are multitaskers. I come from a family where men are patriarchal." Arora adds, "My dad was the first guy to break the rules and have my mom work and raise his daughters to work."

Living Our Own Lives

Harini Calamur is 50 years old, living with her dog outside of Pune, working for a global company. Calamur decided to never marry and live a life on her own terms as an empowered single woman. "I grew up seeing all women working a great deal. Working at home, at the office, going out for groceries. Everywhere. As someone who grew up watching them, I asked myself if this is the life I really want. Is this empty life of silence and pass-me-the-salt what I really want. I saw cousins, aunts, uncles and they had big fights on many random things—who should be PM, who is getting married, who is dead. Almost seemed like there was nothing in common except two people sharing a roof. I didn't see interaction." Witnessing marriages around her that lacked balance and happiness made

Harini question the entire concept of marriage. Do women really need marriage?

"I saw the wrong couples. Maybe there are happy couples," she says. Adding further, "Only reason I would have gone through marriage was if I wanted to be a mother."

I ask her if the institution of marriage should be up for debate. "Nothing is wrong with it. It's an institution that's age old. In the 21st century it needs to be redefined. It's a great way of having legal heirs but unless there is a definite reason for you to get married, I don't think it makes sense. You are talking of extraordinary commitment, extraordinary long lives."

The history of marriage as a concept has been problematic from the very beginning. As per some evidence, marriages date back over 4,000 years and originated as a concept of social contract with little to do with love or even religion. A detailed article in *The Week* notes, "...marriage's primary purpose was to bind women to men, and thus guarantee that a man's children were truly his biological heirs. Through marriage, a woman became a man's property."

From then to now, what's not changed is the belief that women need to be "protected" and that men should wield power over them. As women seek change, they realise that some of the most powerful tools to unshackle them from such historic unwritten societal binds is to find independence—physical, emotional, financial, and intellectual.

And so, in a world where women stand their own ground, feel safe and secure, and lead careers, why should marriage be necessary? Marriage may only be an option for those who choose to exercise it.

Rebecca Traister in her book, *All The Single Ladies,* mentions the "culturally enforced" weight of comparing love, marriage, and motherhood to "femininity". It's a powerful observation. When women try to make the shift from femininity to "profession" which she defines as intellectual freedom, money, and recognition, they are faced with resistance. Society questions women who want to crossover or have both. It equally ridicules a woman who chooses to drop femininity for profession.

"Women are not allowed to be financially independent because they are expected to be dependent and are expected to serve another household for the rest of their life," says Calamur. "She is getting into a marriage because someone will look after her because she was never given an opportunity to stand on her own two feet."

For Calamur, who lives with her dog, Cookie, singlehood is "the exuberance of being yourself".

"Singlehood is something I approach with joy. I cannot imagine not being single. It's the exuberance of being yourself." For her, marriage is a self-less affair. Each person involved in it is expected to make significant sacrifices to make the marriage work.

For some reason, marriages are always looked at as financial security for women, but why not as financial deprivation asks Calamur.

"Financial independence is only a part of it. Being in a marriage is a financial deprivation too. The amount of sacrifice we have to do for each other, for the families is phenomenal. Yes, they don't think of it as a sacrifice but privilege. People give up hobbies, going out, travelling etc for their families and kids."

Increasingly, the joys of singlehood are not just the sacrifices one can skip but the space one gets to enjoy. In most Indian marriages, it's assumed a woman has sacrificed her sense of space and time for the "greater good" of the family. Calamur picks a simple example to make a strong point about absence of privacy for the female and a right to know for the man.

"The concept of privacy within a marriage is not a given thing. When a man gets an SMS, a woman can hardly ask him who is it from. But a man feels it's his right to know."

Ketaki Sathe is a marketing consultant who lives in Mumbai with two children. Divorced, she is 40 and a triathlon runner.

Her love for public relations made her experiment with her own consultancy. "That part of my career has developed in the four years after my divorce." Before her separation, she was part of her husband's family business which she says "didn't inspire" her at all.

"I graduated college in Bangalore and started work in PR. Decided to go abroad after marrying my husband, whose business was engaged with the Pharma industry. I used to take my first child to the factory by building a nursery there. But this work was not stimulating me."

"It was a home business, it didn't feel like a great job to be in. I wanted to have a job that paid better. I was getting paid but I knew I could get paid more if I was out of the family business."

While marriages are about mutual support among many other things, one has to draw a line on "to be someone who isn't just the support for a partner. And do what is expected of you for the greater good of the family." By the time Ketaki had her second child, she quit the family business to turn entrepreneur and set up a business in toys. This was also around the time when her marriage was showing first signs of cracks. But this entrepreneurial stint, even though it wound up in two years, taught her a lot about financial independence.

When a woman separates from her husband, she is put through many questions and conversations on "how" she will manage.

"I was able to manage my insurance, my investments, file my own taxes. Women are not raised to learn this. We leave this to the husbands," she says with confidence. "I recently bought a bike worth a couple of lakhs, and I didn't have to answer to anyone."

Now in Mumbai, she looks back at her decisions and believes they were the right ones. "I was asked if I would move back to Bangalore to be with family when we separated. It wasn't an option. I wanted to be in the city where my ex-husband was. We split the holidays. We are open with the kids. The father comes more often. For us the kids are central—we are co-parenting."

Sathe realised that to have a balanced life for herself and the children, it was important that she made time for her career and that could only happen if the two parents stayed in the same city and shared responsibility.

For her, running has been a hobby for the last two decades and one that helped her chart out her course as a single mom as well. "Running was my getaway in the worst of my times. It helped me focus and centre myself. It helped me stand up for myself. Earlier, I ran at night after putting my babies to bed. I would take any time I would get but I had to get that run in." Shortly after her divorce, Sathe took up her two passions—PR and running even more aggressively. "Very serendipitously I stumbled into the world of triathlons. I had access to pools, a cycle, and all these disciplines meant I didn't only have to go out in the morning but could find a small window at other times of the day and dedicate time for myself. I got a babysitter who came at 5 am and managed my kids while I trained. It taught me I could do things for which I had no confidence. I am racing with road bikes, I have done swimathons in the ocean, it has been mentally helpful in a difficult personal stage of life—when you are separating, negotiating, and finding closure." Even as women find their calling and independence, India's societal construct remains intrusive and interfering—sometimes directly and often indirectly.

Housing for Single Women

Ad film director Shikha Makan's telling documentary *Bachelor Girls* highlights the plight of single women wanting to rent a house in Mumbai. Makan arrived in the "city of dreams" to work in the film industry but struggled to find housing because she was "single" and landlords felt single women "invite trouble".

"Do you drink or smoke? Do you go out late at night? Boys will not be allowed. Tell us if you have a boyfriend," these were among the routine questions

Makan and the women she interviewed for the documentary experienced.

This is despite the fact that among Indian cities, Mumbai is where women feel most safe. The buzzing metropolis is home to professionals across sectors working late, using public transport, and making a living. It's the city where Bollywood is and a large number of women are employed in the business.

"The prism through which our society views a woman is tinted with judgments about character, clothes, lifestyle, and personal life," says Makan about her research on the documentary.

In fact, sometimes, women are forced to lie and pretend they are married in order to get housing. "I got my first job in Mumbai with a bank but for four months I stayed with my aunt because no one would rent out to me. I finally had to lie about being married, before I landed up a one-bedroom studio. I couldn't believe I had no choice," shares Radhika.

Single mothers don't have it any different. A mother of one, who wanted to remain anonymous, and runs her own business, said she could not rent out a house in Delhi because she is a single parent. "I had just moved to Delhi back then and wanted to live in a more spacious house with my mother and daughter and so I started my hunt for a house to rent. However, I came to know that people were anxious to rent a house to me because I am a woman and once when somebody did rent out an apartment to me, within six months they started creating problems and wanted us to move out. I didn't face this in Bangalore but in Delhi it was very apparent."

Finding a home can be the starting point of independence for women. Whether it's in the form of a safe space or from where they head to work every single day, living independently brings an empowering sense of not having to depend on someone else for one's survival. Inheritance and property rights in India were amended a few years ago to include the rights of daughters.

However as a society, we need to make this change in how we perceive single women. A deep discussion on policies by government to improve housing access can be an important shift in recognising and enabling the economic opportunities for women.

The United Nations Human Rights Office notes that, "The right to adequate housing is a central component of women's right to equality under international human rights law." As a result of discrimination and inequality in housing, many women and girls live in insecure, undignified and unsafe conditions, at increased risk of homelessness and violence.

Why Aren't We Banking on Women?

Forty-seven-year-old Anubha Bhonsle walked into a bank to get a home loan. A journalist, with a good credit history, she has held many senior positions in media and is financially independent for the last 20 years. "They wouldn't give me a loan," says Anubha who divorced her husband a few years ago and went to seek the loan for herself, by herself.

"As someone who had a house to her name, a great credit score, I was asked to go get a no-objection certificate from my younger brother just because I was taking on a financial responsibility and so just in case I didn't meet it, they would have my younger brother to sign off." These are the kind of "everyday reminders" women in India face. "Even when I went to get a visa, and ticked divorce on the form, I would have to give many explanations."

The Indian banking system doesn't discriminate on gender but the perceived understanding of the manager behind the counter can be a big influencing factor in who gets a loan.

The Convenience of It

Experiences like Anubha's force women to think of the practicality of being single too.

"I got married at 22, I was divorced at 22 and nine months," says Jasmine, who is now 41. "I spent two years of my life after the divorce getting my documents fixed." In India, as in many other parts of the world, women change their surname (and sometimes their first name too) after getting married.

"All my tax documents, all my identity cards, all were a mess. I had lost myself in my husband's surname and struggled to get rid of it," she says of India's complex system for revising your identity details. "Even now I find myself on Google with two different surnames and it's very unnerving."

Women choosing to be single parents: Why can't we accept that?

As women are increasingly raising their voice against injustices within the family, cases of separation in marriages are also rising and it's only for the good. This pattern is also adding to the number of single parents in the country. A recent report conducted by UN Women revealed cases of women in various kinds of homes like homes run by couples, couples living with children, extended families etc, and single mothers running their homes to gauge the progress of women within these types of homes. In its research it found that India alone comprises approximately 13 million single mothers running their homes, making it around an estimated 4.5% of all Indian households in the country.

What Do the Numbers Say?

The recently released report titled "Progress of the World's Women 2019–2020: Families in a Changing World" examines how the transformations in families impact women's rights and reveals that most countries can afford family-friendly policies. It found that globally a vast majority of lone-parent families, which are 8% of households, are led by women, often juggling paid work, child-rearing, and unpaid domestic work.

According to the Sample Registration Report of 2018, released last year, 5.5% of women in India live alone. Kerala (9.3%) and Tamil Nadu (9.2%) account for the highest number of single women living alone in the country. Moreover, the report added, "The proportion of widowed/divorced/separated women is higher than that of men in all states and Union Territories." But, according to a UN Women report, in India, the poverty rate of single mothers is equal to 38% while for dual-parent households it is 22.6%.

"Around the world, we are witnessing concerted efforts to deny women's agency and their right to make their own decisions in the name of protecting 'family values'. Yet, we know through research and evidence that there is no 'standard' form of family, nor has there ever been," said UN Women Executive Director, Phumzile Mlambo-Ngcuka. "This report counters that push back by showing that families, in all their diversity, can be critical drivers of gender equality, provided decision-makers deliver policies rooted in the reality of how people live today, with women's rights at their core."

These statistics recorded over the past years indicate that single women and single mothers constitute a significant population in our country. But their empowerment and acceptance still lie in the fringes of the country's social attitudes and policies. Despite constituting a significant presence in the nation, single women are excluded from the normative as helpless, weak or bechari women. Their independence and happiness is not valued as much as that of single men, even though the population of single women exceeds that of single men. The laws and policies of the stakeholders are not inclusive of the concerns and rights of single women. Presence of and dependence on husbands is often made mandatory for single women to have an easy and respectable life in Indian society.

When single women form such a large group of the country's population, doesn't it make sense to include their needs, rights, and voices in the policies that are formulated? Shouldn't society and its stakeholders put an effort towards making the country a better place for single women to live and thrive?

Young Single Mothers Are Judged for Their Success

While many single mothers live alone, there are also those who live in their extended families. However, the conventional South Asian patriarchal society does not spare single mothers of prejudices, misconceptions, and judgements. Nidhi Shirim, who works as an executive assistant at a well-recognised construction company in Ahmedabad spoke to *SheThePeople* about being a single mother and dealing with success. "Being a single parent and a woman, we still have to deal with the taboos in society. If the woman is successful in her profession then the first thing that comes to people's minds is that there has to be something fishy about it, especially if you are a young single mother.

"If there is a young male single parent, he would be lauded for it but just because I am a woman, a lot of people judge me on the basis of my success. There have been several occasions I have received judgemental looks from people if they saw me sitting with my male colleagues or friends. It affects my mental health and makes me feel like I have done something wrong by accessing the workplace."

She added that while on this front not much has changed in the society at the mindset level, she has also faced issues in getting official work done. "Once I wanted to start an investment scheme at the post office for my daughter and for documentation of the scheme called 'Sukanya', they required the father's signature on it. I told them that I am a single parent and had divorced right at that time, and then they wanted to have my degree. I also told them that I have not received my degrees from my matrimonial house but they refused to approve my application."

Dating for Single Women in India

Dating and remarriage in India is looked down upon for a divorced mother more than for a widowed mother.

Paromita, a single mom to two, lives in Kolkata. She is a teacher and sent her children to boarding schools. Paromita, 42, says that there would be no issues with a single father dating because people sympathise with them but when it comes to women, it is extremely difficult. "It's not an issue abroad but the society here is such that single mothers feel suffocated."

Priyanka Sehgal, who founded the dating app Sparkles, says, "We need to encourage youngsters and people who are divorced, for instance, to find ways and means to get to the right partner by evaluating them through different circumstances and experiences."

"I did this mostly to solve a problem for myself," Sehgal says. For someone whose social life had taken a backseat and who had never dated before, meeting new people after her divorce brought forth some revelations.

Has the Condition of Single Mothers Changed Over the Years?

Speaking about the changes that have happened over the years, Anita Aggarwal, who has been a single mother for over two decades now, believes that things have gotten better for women today but patriarchal thoughts persist. "With education and awareness we have come a long way, now that women have started earning a livelihood, they don't feel as downtrodden as women during my time. And with time, you start ignoring a lot of things said about you but the one thing that comes out of it is that you teach your children to never settle in the face of injustice.

"I remember feeling like I have stolen something big for living separately with my mother at my parents' place. I also didn't have the kind of education women are exposed to today because in those days a lot of women did not study professional degrees because they were never expected to earn a living. But I still made use of what my education allowed me and that's what one has to rely upon. No one else other than your family comes to your support, and that's why one mustn't pay heed to society."

Ketaki agrees with this. "I am still dealing with this bechari factor. When I separated I was 40. There was social ostricisation, there were friends who I thought were mine, but they chose to go away. And then there were those who judged me and my decision."

"She is ok she is wearing lipstick, she looks fine"—things Ketaki Sathe has heard. "It's been hard. People feel uncomfortable having single women around at home when their husbands are there," she says. "We meet for coffee outside. I don't need that energy in my life. I have made many good friends within sports. We have similar routines. There has been a shift for me in the social space. People look at you funny, you learn to ignore it. If as a single woman you wear dresses, or wear shorts or seem confident, you get judged.

"I am judged by other mothers. They feel awkward.

But what matters is my own family and my kids are okay, cause I am okay."

Sathe has recognised how society pulls women down and coming to terms with it has meant a lot more confidence and peace. "Half the time I am self-counselling, or I am venting with my mom, a lot of our time goes in meeting expectations, putting up a brave front, feeding to society's needs. Imagine a world without judgement, without my back story—I would work to my potential."

Stories and anecdotes of the women in this chapter should draw our attention towards understanding how singlehood can be an opportunity for women to be economically empowered. Women in our society are bred to be dependent on their fathers first and then their husbands for their financial needs. But, when women are single and on their own, they push themselves to achieve financial education and empowerment. Rather than depending on a man for their needs, women understand the importance of their own independence. They don't feel inferior to men who have the power to make decisions and earn and manage money. They not only become their own leaders but also encourage other women to envision a life that is different from the traditions set by patriarchy.

A single earning woman is the most powerful person in a patriarchal society. She threatens every system that holds a woman back—with her guts and money. All that needs to be done is to provide them a support system so that rather than dealing with unwanted gendered tribulations, single women can focus on being better each day. And if more and more single women, who constitute a large group of the country's population, seek financial independence, India's GDP and economic position will also see new heights. Therefore, it will not be wrong to say that accepting and empowering single women can prove to be India's major opportunity to meet its economic goals. It is about time that women should be conditioned to prioritise their empowerment and independence over social expectations which are old, gendered, and wrong. So, how do we normalise singlehood for women? It's going to take a shift in our mindsets and societal expectations, but perhaps we can start taking the first steps—design policies that don't question a women's single status, create support structures for single parents, and build an ecosystem that helps them thrive economically, emotionally, and professionally.

It is a demographic that is quietly asserting its right to be taken seriously, and creating its own space, whether it's through films, books, clubs, or conversations. It's time we stood up and took notice.

chapter eleven

Technology Can Change the Game?

Madhuri Balodi's hobby was to craft home décor items. She started with a regular 9–5 day job to meet her financial needs. But later, she quit her job to take a dive into entrepreneurship when her hobby began occupying most of her time. She started The Kavi Project which recycles things to make quirky home décor products and sold them at the many flea markets and bazaars. But when COVID-19 hit the world, most offline businesses were impacted due to the uncertain periods of lockdowns. But Balodi didn't give up. She expanded her business to the digital platform by opening an e-commerce website and linking up with major portals to sell her artworks. She came in touch with international shopping sites and turned those into goals for her business. "Large digital platforms like YouTube, Facebook can be good for promotions as well as help in increasing the sales if you use these mediums to grow your business." Clearly digital was helping her big time.

Masoom Minawala is a digital content creator with millions of followers on Instagram. She used the internet to take Indian clothes to global fashion runways. Minawala has built an empire on social media after an early dabble with a blog she created called Style Fiesta, one of the first e-commerce portals in India. Minawala's career peak comes after 15 tough years of building content she believed in and at a time when few were willing to take her seriously.

"The funny thing is that people think it happened overnight, but I think my case has been a case of slow and steady. I wouldn't say that wins the race because I don't believe in winning the race. I believe I am my biggest competition. But the thing is, I don't look at fame, but I'd say I have reached where I am today after many years of consistently doing what I'm doing. So, honestly it didn't happen overnight, it wasn't that easy and definitely not that quick."

Creators like Minawala are not just putting their best foot forward but also taking the rest along. "This is where I saw that somebody like me can play a very important role, especially in the middle and I was like, how do I leverage this platform I have to help and support thousands of these small businesses who are possibly and probably going to shut shop because they can't deal with the pandemic and the effect that pandemic has on their businesses, which actually was the reason that my series 'Support Indian Designers' began."

Madhuri Balodi and Masoom Minawala are examples of those who have kickstarted a new wave of development and modernisation. Through its advanced ways of connecting, communicating, and availing various services, digital opportunities are making India one of the leading cosmopolitan countries in the world.

Digitalisation has not only improved education, communication and other daily activities but has also boosted the economy. Even though India's start-up story is often criticised for being inflated at times, and money comes and goes, there are many important and breakthrough businesses that have emerged that have brilliantly leveraged the digital.

At the heart of this, is how digital tools are empowering women in rural and urban areas. There are national programmes for this, and many different platforms are working on providing easier access to women's health, digital learning and upskilling, and more.

The Internet Saathi Impact Study conducted by TNS in 2018 shows that through the programme 70% of women in rural areas were able to use the internet for the first time. By 2018, 60,000 Internet Saathis across various states in India were successful in imparting digital literacy to 20 million women across 200,000 villages. That's one such program and then there are many others.

At the age of five, Shalu Devi from Punjab lost her legs due to polio. But this did not deter her from her aim to empower herself. After marriage, she started stitching basic patchwork bedsheets for ₹50 and teaching children who could not go to schools. Later when she received access to the internet, she learnt to stitch women's salwar-suits and men's shirts. Today, she is able to get enough orders to generate a good revenue. She is also able to employ others through her earnings.

When her husband walked out of the marriage, Mustan Kaur from Punjab started earning her own living by cleaning others' houses. Later, with the support of the village council and friends, she started a canteen in a women's college. She used the internet to learn to cook new dishes and sell them in the canteen. "I turned to the internet to learn many new dishes that were popular in other canteens. There are so many videos that show you how to make a single dish and I would spend my free time poring over those. I have now perfected burgers, samosas, and chinese noodles at my canteen and these are our best selling items. Business has really taken off," she says.

SheThePeople, which has the largest community of women entrepreneurs, has been hosting the globally acclaimed Digital Women Awards and Summit to spotlight young women breaking new ground with entrepreneurship across different sectors. The mission is to continue to build this platform for future leaders who will shape the Indian digital ecosystem and the women who build it. These stories are ground realities of how digitalisation is helping women to gain a stand in society. It is working as a best friend for women to enable themselves despite all the obstacles.

As per a report by Accenture, "If governments and businesses can double the pace at which women become digitally fluent, we could reach gender equality in the workplace by 2040 in developed nations and by 2060 in developing nations." Women are truly the workforce waiting to be tapped.

Digital Brings Voice to Women

Whether through an Instagram channel or a video, digital content creation has given a voice to women. Some are sharing their crochet designs, others are questioning stereotypes. In a sense, digitalisation has offered women opportunities to educate and empower themselves from the comfort of their homes.

During the COVID-19 pandemic, education and upskilling is also happening via the internet, WhatsApp, and other tools. Perhaps a few decades down the line education will be and feel different. It has completely transformed the meaning of education and made it more interesting, interactive, and approachable than ever before—with visualisation tools and other social media.

Sapangeet Rajwant, an award-winning marketer with more than two decades of experience in India's entertainment industry, notes, "...that mobile and digital technologies offer women the potential to bypass some of the traditional cultural and mobility barriers, particularly in emerging and developing countries like ours. Digital technologies could help women access new markets, work flexibly and distantly, acquire and interact with customers, receive training and provide mentoring, improve financial autonomy, and access finance for their ventures."

The internet also offers to bridge the gap in critical information. Advocate Manasi Chaudhari came up with Pink Legal, an online portal for women that aims to have all the information on women's legal rights.

"Although we have a number of laws for the

benefit of women, most of them do not even know that these laws exist. What is surprising is that even urban, educated women are not aware of their legal rights," says Chaudhari in an interview. She also adds, "Pink Legal wants to bridge this gap by bringing the law to women and explaining all women-related laws in a very simple manner. The laws are organised into relevant topics, like sexual harassment, domestic violence, etc., so that women can understand all the laws which cover these topics, in one go."

Starting Something of Their Own

Many women have used social media to sell their crafts online and become entrepreneurs. Digitalisation has played a vital role in increasing the number of women entrepreneurs in urban and rural India. According to a recent report,* the business owned by women entrepreneurs in India will grow by 90% in the next five years.

Especially during the pandemic, women entrepreneurs who were working offline got on the internet to expand their business.

"Doing something you love is happiness, but getting paid for something you love doing is a blessing," says Anjalee Das, the founder of Cookiee and Craft that makes vintage photo frame art, handcrafted vintage envelopes, junk journals, gift hampers, and many more things. Once, she displayed her art on the

*https://timesofindia.indiatimes.com/business/india-business/women-owned-businesses-in-india-to-rise-90-in-next-5-years-report/articleshow/82101858.cms

internet and was astonished by the good response that her work received. "That's when my hobby turned into my profession, which led me to the world of entrepreneurship."

However, when the pandemic hit the world, her business met a roadblock. "Things were difficult and a lot more challenging during the lockdown not only with respect to health but also with respect to the business. As the economy of the country came to a halt, craft supplies were not available, people were not ready to buy something which is non-essential," Das said. But she used this time to grow her business online.

Srinia Chowdhury is a trained sculptor who showcases unconventional ideas and views about the society she lives in on mugs and other art pieces. She has taken her art for exhibition in various art galleries and has amassed immense success. Now she is handcrafting her works not just for admiration but to sell to people for daily use. And that's how the journey of Chowdhury as an artpreneur began. "I decided to go become an artpreneur because I realised my art is reaching the masses and there is a crowd who actually appreciates using functional art which is purely handmade and not blindly mass-produced," she says.

However, when the pandemic hit the world, her business too went on a roller coaster. But Chowdhury managed to hold her balance by expanding her business to the online world. "During COVID like a lot of people, I studied some business techniques, I had to incorporate them in my unique way as an artist. That is a challenge we all face as artists! For some reason, art colleges do not teach the business side. So, I had to polish my own skills to come out as an artist-entrepreneur," she says. Today she has not only set up her own studio but also a webshop for her artwork. "During the pandemic, I realised that I have to push myself to launch my webshop to keep relevant with the changing times to showcase my art." She also adds, "I realised the power of digital during COVID. Now everything is online and that encouraged me to re-launch my portfolio-only website with a webshop and to the good grace of the universe, it got an amazing response."

Prachi Buchar, a policy expert working in the field of technology, reflects on how good-tech impacts women in small towns. "Everyone keeps talking about digital transformation but to see what it truly is, you need to venture beyond the cities. Young women in small towns, even villages, are choosing to build careers by leveraging the power of the internet to create a small income for themselves."

One doesn't have to be educated as skills come handy. Scores of women across India are learning basic internet behaviour and upskilling on using the internet for themselves and their families and businesses. Buchar adds, "You don't need to be educated or have a lot of money to invest, the digital economy allows you to test waters through something as simple as your phone. We are a country of women hungry for change, hungry for acceptance, and hungry to tap into a changing India and this is apparent when you travel down the line to rural areas."

Striking a Balance?

Some argue the internet has also helped working women in maintaining the balance between home and office. Online shopping of groceries, home delivery of safe and healthy food, parenting tips, online availability of cleaning services, and many other such things have helped women to manage their time well and focus on their jobs. There is however also that other argument that work from home has blurred boundaries between work, home, and children for women giving them excess work.

UK-based financial journalist, Katerine Marcel, says that it will give us an opportunity to reassess the economy and account for the unpaid care work done by women. In an interview, she says that economists have concluded that many of the jobs that men have been doing traditionally will be taken over by machines and robots in the digital age. "While", she adds, "many of the things women have specialised in like emotional intelligence, they are not at all likely to be taken over by machines." Marcel points out that though unpaid care work has always been rendered feminine and hence less valuable and important, it will gain importance through digitalisation and humans, and not women alone, will be specialising in care work.

Bridging the Divide

These are some questions that need to be addressed to make the digital age truly a new wave of women's participation. It is undeniable that there is an existing gender divide in access to the internet and technologies. The fifth National Family Health Survey revealed that only 42% of Indian women surveyed have ever used the internet as compared to 62% of men. In rural areas, the number drops further with only 34% of women and 55% of men having internet access.

Even in the case of the gig economy, there is an evident gender gap. The ratio of men and women working in the gig economy is 50:50. The new employment opportunities generated by the gig economy has been gendered. It has made women vulnerable by confining them to highly stigmatised jobs like beauty services or formalised care work like nannies. In the gig economy, men earn 7% more per hour than women.

There is also a dearth of academic research in the concerns, labour practices, and organisation of informal women workers which include the gig workers and women in small businesses, among others.

These statistics clearly show the prevalence of a stark gender gap in the access to internet and technology. According to a study of 2019, if the gender gap in the digital sector persists, it will reduce women's participation in labour which will be counted on the basis of technological adoption in the future. If women lack internet access, how will the digital age's promise to bridge the gender gap ever reach its goal?

It is important to note here that there is a general disagreement in society about women using mobile phones and the internet. In the past few years, we have come across several comments, that too from prominent leaders of the country, that women should not be allowed to use mobile phones and the internet to keep them safe from sexual harassment. It is assumed that women who are active on social media are not sanskari enough.

This is again the major reason why women who voice their opinions on social media platforms are slut-shamed by trolls. Many women are subjected to online abuse and harassment which makes it difficult for women to be active in the digital world. Cases of trolling, rape threats, morphed photos, cyberbullying and many more have been on the rise ever since the internet gained importance in our lives.

Enabling Their Girls at Home

Despite all the awareness and widespread conversation, many Indian families buy a smartphone and internet connection only for their sons. Women are excluded because their empowerment is not valued as much. Last year, *SheThePeople* came across Radhika, a teacher at a government-aided school in Delhi who has been taking online classes for her students ever since schools closed due to lockdown. In the initial days of taking these classes, while she was still adjusting to the entire process, she came across a family of three daughters and one son that was reluctant to allow their daughters to attend the lectures. They said that it was difficult to pay for the internet connection of four kids. And since girls have to ultimately marry into other families, their education is not important enough.

So for women to fully benefit from digitalisation, there is a need to overcome the general biases prevalent in society. Women need to be provided with equal, free and proper access to technology and the internet, and should be taught about their rights in the digital world. They should be told about cybercrimes and how they can approach cyber cells for help. For this, the cyber cell also needs to be active in addressing the cases of online harassment.

Digitalisation surely promises a bright future for women. But it should not be at the cost of their safety and equal rights. Digitalisation will become another medium to oppress and exclude women if the gender stereotypes behind it are not addressed in time.

chapter twelve

Caste in Stone

Caste is more than just a word in India. It is the identity of a person. It determines the legitimacy of a person. And it carves out the life that the person is destined to live. Our country is marred by the social evil of caste inequality. Dalits and other backward classes are pushed to the fringes of society just because they have taken birth in a different community. The marginalised castes are suppressed by the upper castes, socially and economically. Practices like untouchability and caste violence have oppressed the marginalised sections historically and these practices continue in our society. Our religious scriptures legitimise caste inequality which then reflects in the economic systems of our society too.

Those from marginalised sections are denied proper education and employment and are forced to do menial jobs with low earnings while the high-paid jobs still remain with upper caste people. According to a report* of 2012, upper caste households earn 47% more than the national average household income. While the scheduled castes, scheduled tribes, and other backward classes earn 21%, 34% and 8% less than the national average. Hence, caste plays a significant role in determining the class of a person which is an economical division of families based on their income.

But when we talk about caste inequality, we cannot ignore the factor of gender. Caste and gender inequality go hand in hand. While caste inequality oppresses people on the basis of birth, gender inequality oppresses people on the basis of their gender. The worst brunt of caste and gender inequality is borne by lower caste women whose life becomes a manifestation of the worst intersection of caste and gender inequality. Women of marginalised castes are oppressed in society not just because of their lower caste but subservient gender too. Women belonging to lower castes, especially Dalit women, are oppressed by the patriarchs within their community *and* the patriarchs of the upper castes, while upper caste men embody the most powerful position in the society—because of their caste and gender.

The double discrimination of Dalit women leads to various issues like lack of opportunities and sexual and mental harassment. In the past few years, Dalit women have been subject to sexual violence at the hands of upper caste men quite frequently. Rape and abduction of Dalit women are often used as a tool by upper caste men to suppress or punish the Dalit

---

*https://wid.world/document/n-k-bharti-wealth-inequality-class-and-caste-in-india-1961-2012/

family or the woman herself. The Dalit women's bodies embody the honour of the family, community, and caste. Their bodies become the ground of caste-based violence in our society.

Aditi Narayani, a Dalit author, writes in *SheThePeople* that the caste system is a hierarchical setting in which the privileges and freedom accrue to the top strata of the system and which successively dies down, leaving the bottom strata (the untouchables) with hardly anything to go by. "The status of communities as 'untouchables' in the Hindu rank framework was the most serious obstruction for the empowerment of Dalit women. While stringent social taboos conscribed their conduct, serious structures were set down to limit their entrance to information. Dalit women have been the most exceedingly terrible sufferers in the exploitative social request."

As per India's national crime bureau report of 2019, the rate of crimes against Dalits has risen by 37% in the last one decade while the conviction rate of such crimes has decreased by 2.5%. Ten cases of rape were reported daily in India last year with Rajasthan reporting the highest number of rapes (554 cases). Rajasthan was followed by Uttar Pradesh with 537 cases, and Madhya Pradesh with 510 rape cases.

The women's movement is greatly affected by both caste and gender inequality. The major reason is the idea that often women enablement or empowerment is defined in terms of the experiences of elite women. The views of women of marginalised classes who obviously have different lived experiences rarely get recorded, understood, and addressed. We cannot forget that feminism began as a movement of white women which made it racist to Black women. Similalrly, the western idea of feminism often fails to address the problems that lower caste women in India face in their lives. Dalit women are denied opportunities because of their caste and gender. Beena Pallical, General Secretary of Dalit Arthik Adhikar Andolan, tells *SheThePeople* that leadership within feminist movements have always been from a privileged point of view. Dalit women are rarely provided with leadership opportunities.

Poet Meena Kandasamy condenses this to an important question in an interview with *The Guardian*—"Who is the narrator, who is allowed to tell the story?" The author, who has articulated Dalit suffering in many of her works including *The Gypsy Goddess*, and *Exquisite Cadavars* among others, addresses issues of caste and untouchability—something that stems from her being a Dalit and being a woman. "This gatekeeping is along the lines of inequalities: caste and class and gender and race," she says.

"It is not just saying, 'women are equal to men'—it goes beyond that to say, 'Look, the caste system is rotten', 'Look, language is unequally constructed', and asks difficult questions," Kandasamy asserts in a talk with Pen Transmissions.

In many cases, the feminist movement that is believed to embody ideals of gender equality becomes questionable. If feminism is always addressed from the perspective of upper caste women, it will be biased and never truly achieve the promised equality. Dalit women will remain oppressed, and not only by men but women too who ignore the factor of caste in women empowerment. Bahujan and Adivasi feminists, for example, would admit that many elite and Dalit feminists have common views, conceptions, and misconceptions about Bahujans (currently* clubbed as part of other backward classes).

The struggle at every layer of caste is real and it gets worse for women in these groups. It is thus important to make feminism intersectional. It is important to understand empowerment from the perspective of Dalit women who will need a different kind of enabling structure to eliminate the double discrimination that they face. They need to defy not only the gender norms but the caste division too in order to be empowered women in the true sense.

"Everything is clear in the law, on the paper, but we are having to fight to retain what is ours," says lawyer Kiruba Munusamy.

For women who are online, the backlash and hate is more vicious and gendered but for those from Dalit and other castes, this worsens to an appalling level. Munusamy shares, "Women who are vocal are being abused for their freedom of expression or choice of dressing. But the kind of abuse I face is peculiar. A woman who doesn't even identify with her caste, gets rape threats and they will say something like you don't even deserve to be raped." She also notes, among the many gaps in support and a sisterhood for women from lower castes is that not only do men discriminate

---

*https://www.impriindia.com/wp-content/uploads/2021/04/Lata-Pratibha-Madhukar_Jaatibhed-or-lingbhed-key-karan-pitrasattta-ki-samaj-pr-pakad_April_2021.pdf

but women too are part of that castiest behaviour and distance themselves or directly discriminate against women from Dalit and other lower castes.

To an extent, the genesis of this lies in what Isabel Wilkerson calls purity versus pollution. She notes in her book *Caste* that there is a "fundamental belief in the purity of the dominant caste and the fear of pollution from the castes deemed beneath it". She documents that in India, "...lowest caste people were to remain a certain number of paces from any dominant caste person while walking out in public. They had to wear bells to alert those deemed above them so as not to pollute them with their presence."

Bell Hooks notes in *Feminism: A Movement to End Sexist Oppression*, "When feminism is defined in such a way that it calls attention to the diversity of women's social and political reality, it centralizes the experiences of all women, especially the women whose social conditions have been least written about, studied, or changed by political movements."

Generally, feminists fight for women's right to get educated and be employed. But Dalit women and those from other discriminated castes, in most of the cases, are already employed in small jobs like domestic help, manual scavenging and more. But this doesn't mean they are empowered. They still need the basic equality within homes, a respectful job, the opportunity to be educated and the right to raise their voices against wrongdoings. So for feminism to achieve the promised equality, it is important to include the lens of caste. Once this is done, empowerment and feminism will not remain the domain of elite women alone. It will become the voice of all women across caste, class and culture. As General Secretary at National Campaign on Dalit Human Rights, Beena Pallical rightly says, "Feminism to me is the right to be yourself. It's more about equity than equality. The right to live with freedom irrespective of caste, class, or gender."

chapter thirteen

Show Me the Money, Honey

When I was growing up, we lived in large chunks in a city called Gwalior in Madhya Pradesh, where we had many months of hot summers in a year. Many of these were marred with prolonged electricity cuts. My dad would use this down time in darkness to ask my sister and me questions and gauge where we were going with our ambitions and dreams, and if we had any. On one such evening in August, with no sight of rain, dad asked me what I wanted to be. I randomly replied, "I want to run my own factory and earn my own money." My dad, a military officer and an airforce fighter pilot, was sort of amused so he asked me why my ambition wasn't to see the world, and explore jobs—like an air hostess'—that took me around?

"Dad, I want to see the world but it will be on my own terms," I apparently quipped. "If I get my own money, I will see the world, won't I?" Over the decades that went by, I turned into a broadcast journalist and rose through the ranks breaking big stories and growing a credible reputation for myself. And I made money. This is how that journey really began.

When I was in college, my dad—a guy with a middle-class salary—said he would cover tuition and hostel fees but I would have to earn my fun-time and anything else money by myself. I did summer jobs three times a summer and sold stuff that went from American Express charge cards to newly introduced cleaning sprays. These odd roles paid me like ₹600 to ₹1200 an hour back in 1999. My parents had raised me to believe no job is too low and no job too cool. They wanted me to learn the true meaning of the dignity of labour and try all kinds of jobs.

At 18, I was privileged in a way, having seen 10 foreign countries, lived in different cities, and changed 17 schools over these 12 classes owing to my dad's transferable postings. But one thing I learnt and learnt hard was that earning your own money was liberating and important. By the time I graduated out of college I had done seven different summer jobs and written for three newspapers. As an economics honours graduate who got very bored in that course, now I had an alternate profession thanks to these many summer jobs—that of writing and being a journalist. So I took all my savings and bought myself a rover-book (a thick four kilo laptop from the early 2000s) and applied for post graduation with the BBC at the Asian College of Journalism. I topped the broadcast class and landed my first job at CNBC.

I wanted to get that job so bad—the journalism job market was really poor and I was the rare person who actually got a job—that I offered to work at my internship fee for as long as they needed. In less than a couple months into my joining, I had a paid full-time job, I was anchoring on national television, making my own money, and paying my rent and bills. I would be lying if I didn't say it was a big high for me. I was an independent girl who had it under her control. "My own money," I must have said that so many times to the mirror, to myself. Financial freedom isn't about having money. It's about having your own money. So dads, brothers, fathers-in-law, and husbands, don't say "Take as much as you want from me" to the women in your home.

It was that early that I got my first lesson in finance. It was simple. Women and money can be damn good friends. Because they are good for each other. Cut to the 2020s and we are still talking of financial freedom for women. Should it really be a discussion?

A woman in our society is never left free of criticism for whatever she does. If she expects money from men, she is shamed as a gold digger. But if she wants to earn her own money, she is labelled as an unsanskari, rude woman who wants to shame her husband for not being able to provide her with financial support. When cricket entrepreneur and tycoon Lalit Modi tweeted out pictures of him and actor Sushmita Sen, announcing that the two were dating, Sen was trolled and called a gold digger.

Sen, a self-made woman, an actor and a former Miss Universe, lives by the belief, "I buy my own diamonds, I don't need a man for that." A single, unmarried mother of two, Sen has broken many stereotypes in Indian society and film industry. Despite all her success, she became a soft target and was villainised for her personal choice as public and social media chose to suggest that she was interested in the man for his money.

A retired male pilot on social media site, Quora, says that 80% of women in India are gold diggers. He claims that women pretend to be madly in love with men but when it comes to signing prenups, they step back. The person's comment is not shocking when we look at the society that we live in. Because the society we live in has tagged women as those who are always searching for a rich man. Not quite different from hit TV series' like *Bridgerton* or Jane Austen's novels—traditionally, mothers' single-minded obsession is to get their "daughter married off" to a rich suitor.

P Lakshmi lives in Noida, just outside of Delhi. "Shaadi surat dekh kar nahi paisa dekh kar karna (Don't get married looking at the guy's face but his wallet)," she was told from the very beginning by her mother. The concept of a gold digger comes from that very idea. If we bring up girls to believe that their financial independence lies in the hands of the man they marry, how are we going to have emancipation?

Let's reverse the situation, says Deepali Parekh, who is a graduate student from Surat. "When girls are raised to earn their own money, society will tell our moms—who will marry a girl who earns more than her man? My own aunt taunted, 'If you are overqualified how will you find a groom?'" Parekh believes there are many layers to the idea of financial independence.

If society blames women for being gold diggers or

for expecting financial support from men, then it must be fine with women who earn their own money, right? Unfortunately not.

Comedian Kaneez Surka's life goal was to marry. "It was as if I wasn't valid before I got married," says Surka, who was a housewife for three years before she divorced her husband. "After that, it was as if I wasn't valid anymore."

"Women often get into marriages for security. I didn't think I had it in me to financially support myself." Financial freedom helps women like Surka and others escape bad marriages and say no, and that's a very good reason to earn your own money. Since then, Surka has not only built a brilliant career in improv and comedy, she says with great confidence and honesty that opting for marriage again will not be because she "needs" it or because it will bring a sense of "security", instead it will be for love or the relationship.

Anuradha Kuli, 42, runs a saree business in Assam. She grew up in the Dhemaji district and is the bread earner of her family. Growing up, her father got her married into a local politician's family. "Parents see the size of the house when they get you married and not what's going on inside," she says. "This was an arranged marriage and soon after I realised my husband was a pauper and they had lost all their money in standing up for elections."

Kuli, like many Indian women, didn't want to tell her parents about her situation and worry them, so she decided to take up a job. She joined the area's sericulture department. "I had two daughters then, two and three years of age. I had to wake up at 4 am to head to work and I would return in the evening and work at home." Kuli was always interested in the rich textile heritage of Assam. Since the money she earned wasn't enough Kuli set up a loom and would work till the early hours of the morning before leaving again for her office. "For nearly a decade of my life I have slept an average of three or four hours," Kuli says with an emotional quiver. Starting something of her own back in 2006 was not easy but she persisted.

Once Kuli was discovered and connected with the crafts council, her woven sarees reached many iconic women in India including politician Sonia Gandhi, and actors Jaya Bachchan and Kirron Kher. "For a girl who studied in Dibrugarh in Assam and came from a simple family, building this saree business was tough but it was my choice."

Her husband didn't originally support her—felt it was below his dignity to work with her—and was embarrassed that she ran a loom in the house. "But today he is a transformed man. My two daughters are inspired by the work we have done. Our sarees are now exported for non-resident Indians in Dubai, US and Singapore."

Kuli has seen the possibilities. She is a totally different person now and is on top of her game. She recognises what self-earned money means.

Radhika Bharat Ram, founder of the KARM Fellowship, who is on the board of the Indian Craft Council talks about how many new artists are trying to make a living in villages and towns deep inside India. However, for many women, the business and earnings may be theirs but the man controls the money.

Often, women are getting the money, but the bank account is in the name of the husband. Bharat Ram, talking of a 28-year-old artist, says, "Whenever she calls me, her husband is prompting her from the back. 'Paise ki zaroorat hai' (I need money). And insists the money be put in his account." It's only when the council insists that their only option is getting the money in the woman's account that the husband budges a little.

"There is something in our education system that's not going right. I was brought up to manage my own money and accounts. I might not be earning money because I work in the development sector but I am aware and it's not like someone can take me for a ride. We need to teach our children to embrace money and we need to stop considering it a bad word. The mindset that women don't understand money is a fallacy we need to break."

Lack of Women Workforce Participation

According to the Centre for Monitoring Indian Economy, female* labour force participation fell to 9.4% for the period between September and December of 2021. Before that, in 2020, the percentage was already low at 16.1% due to the impact of the pandemic.

Even though according to economists and statistics, the rate of employment among single women significantly increases after they are widowed or

*https://www.business-standard.com/article/current-affairs/as-indian-women-leave-jobs-single-women-keep-working-here-s-why-118062300375_1.html

separated in marriage from 26% in 2005 to 47% in 2011, women are forced to quit their jobs postmarriage and contribute in housework. According to the Economic Survey of 2020,* around 60% of women are involved in household work.

These statistics prove that the number of women in the workforce is dwindling, but what is the reason behind it? One is the fact that the marriage market is obsessed with graduates but gharelu bahus. Grooms' families are now hunting for brides who are educated enough to spell their name and understand modern trends but homely enough to not go out and earn. Actor Lily Singh pointed out in her TED TALK that even though women are being provided with the seat at the table, the table or the seat is wobbly and uncomfortable as they were never built for women in the first place.

Stating the reason why women are opting out of the workforce, Rajiv Anand, deputy managing director at one of India's largest banks, Axis Bank, says, "I think all of us talk about the fact that women are not coming into the workforce. But what are we doing about it? There is this whole issue of patriarchy. I also believe that women don't feel comfortable or safe with the entire environment. They are either choosing to drop out or in some cases they are opting for entrepreneurship.

"I think it is incumbent on all of us to make an equal space on how they will be treated in terms of increments, bonuses, promotions, etc."

---

*https://www.shethepeople.tv/news/women-opt-out-of-workforce-for-unpaid-care-work-economic-survey/

This decaying situation of women's financial independence is despite the fact that women contribute 17% of the GDP in India. And if female labour force participation is increased, women can add up to $700 billion to the country's GDP by 2025. It's this figure I keep talking of.

How Are Things Changing?

Women are noticing the wave of change around them and taking a leap of faith. Digital outlets, the start-up ecosystem, mobile chat rooms with products, work from home opportunities are all strengthening the efforts of those who want to make a beginning on their own. The job market, though forever fluctuating, is opening new avenues for women as new types of opportunities emerge.

Mumbai-based Nayantara Thomas is passionate about making pastries but starting a business took some time. "There have always been doubts and insecurities. The common ones are whether I am getting the monthly cheques or am I making any money at all. The doubt whether this would work out or not is always there," Thomas says. She took the plunge and started her bakery and uses social media for outreach.

In Gurgaon, Chitra Sharma started her catering service with her husband. "When I first started the kitchen, there were a maximum of 10 orders and some days went without any order. I always feared the loss that I could incur and how would I pay my rent and bills?" Sharma says she had to be on top of all budgeting, plans, and returns on investments. Like many start-ups, she had both financial and operational challenges to begin with but also a brilliant learning curve that has prepared her for new opportunities such as starting a new business.

The determination to follow their passion helped Lakshmi and Chitra unfold the ways to deal with the challenges as entrepreneurs. Even in their jobs, women are asking for growth and promotions, trying to shed their shyness in asking for what they actually deserve.

During the COVID-19 pandemic the right to work from home has also been a reason why women are talking more about work. It's not been easy to measure, but the fact that women don't have to step out to seek self-earning opportunities has made them feel more secure.

Sindhu Gangadharan, the first female boss of tech giant, SAP India, says, "People have realised the comfort and possibilities of work from anywhere. This gives a big opportunity for women in terms of going out there and doing what they believe in and even drive the change."

At a seminar with students from Kalinga University in Orissa, nearly all the questions I was asked were about how women find independence and shed fears of aspiring to be rich. More and more young girls are choosing to become financially independent. They are standing on their feet, gaining seats at formal tables, and running their own enterprises. Banks, insurance companies and other male-dominated sectors are taking notice of how women can be an important market, because they spend (or will spend in the future) and their voices as daughters, wives, sisters, and partners are important to any purchase decision.

Bhimtal-based Gauri Singh believes that if she earns, she won't have to be dependent on anyone for money, be it father, brother, or husband. Money will not only give her the power to buy the life she likes but also the strength to stand against the patriarchy surrounding her.

Singh belongs to a small town where women rarely step out and earn for the family. Her family has often said that it is okay for her to quit education and get married because neither education nor employment is necessary for a woman. Her father says, "I will find a rich groom for you who will provide you with everything. Until then I will pay for your needs."

Today she is working at a non-profit organisation earning a decent salary. She aims to expand her horizon, increase her earnings, and be capable of changing society and support her parents as well.

Stories of women who do and earn are infectious. For example, inspired by Lakshmi, her mother too began dreaming of starting something of her own, like making cloth bags given the demand for organic packaging. Lakshmi's mother had spent her entire life asking or stealing money from her husband because he would never offer. She sells a few bags now and her business is slow but that little packet of earnings is more precious than anything she has done so far.

Charu Kumari, who was born in Bihar and shifted to Rajasthan after marriage, was not employed despite being educated. She has completed her masters and appeared for many banking service examinations. But most of her attempts failed. But before she could try further, her parents got her married to a "wealthy" family of Rajasthan. "Shaan se rahegi," said her relatives. But when she reached her marital home, she had to do all the household chores on her own. She started feeling depressed and stuck in an unhappy marriage. However, she didn't give up. She didn't want to be dependent on anyone for her needs. So she worked hard and attained a job in her town. Today, she is working as a chartered accountant with an ample salary. She has gained the freedom to say no to her in-laws if they oppose her or restrict her and gained the freedom to not do the work she doesn't like.

Examples of these women clearly show that financial independence is a key to women's freedom and choices. And they recognise it. But what's really important is that we believe in financial freedom being a fundamental right, one that's included in our education curriculum.

Another matter that must be addressed as women take charge of their own growth and business is how they use that money for securing their future. Anand adds, "The next level of problem is really, once they become economic entities, then what do they do with the money that they earn, what do they do, you know, how do they save?"

Hena Mehta, based in Bangalore, is the co-founder of Basis, an app for urban women and money. "Women seek privacy and autonomy and control of their own money. It's such a big confidence booster and it gives them power over their own lives," she says.

Mehta, a graduate from University of Pennsylvania, was faced with a personal financial crisis when she got selected for the Wharton Business School. For someone who had worked for nearly eight years before business school, she stared at the Wharton tuition fee and wondered how she would pay for it without taking a loan or asking her parents. "I was done asking for money, I had worked for so many years." This was a dilemma. "I hadn't got plans to take a large loan. I wanted to start a company...and taking a loan would have meant I would have to sign up for a high-paying corporate job. It was my wake-up call. I had been saving all my life, but had I invested well, I would not have faced this situation."

Whether you are from a village outside Igatpuri in Maharashtra or aspiring to go to a global business school, what's clear is that money gives women opportunities. "I can make my own decisions and my own mistakes," Mehta puts succinctly.

Anand adds that it is a wrong narrative that women are not good investors. Stating a study, he said that women are better investors than men. "According to Axis Mutual Funds, they are seeing a seven-times increase in the number of women visitors on their websites from January 2020 to October 2021. Similarly, the number of women investors have also increased in the same period by 30%." As long as we are able to demonstrate that women have a good understanding of money and finances, that itself is a beginning. There are enough examples of this.

In rural India too, the efforts are gathering steam. Parul Seth Khanna who works on digital micro-pension inclusion in Asia and Africa aims to encourage non-salaried workers to save for a secure and dignified retirement.

"Women have challenges around financial literacy,

challenges around intermittent income because of family responsibilities, or have lesser incomes to no income at all. However, they always save. They always know how much money they have in their pockets. They save in informal instruments. They don't really go to formal financial institutions as they are intimidated by technology." And that's where the tech gap will be critical to build and change things.

"Technology has become an enabler for women who are seeking financial independence and security. It has made the entire process within reach and easier. Women are able to open bank accounts online, save and invest money with rare cases of discrepancy."

While at one level, India's youth are struggling with understanding money, there are those who are trying to experiment thanks to massive information flow and access on the internet. Many don't want to be restricted by what their neighbourhood banks offer.

This is a story of a woman who wanted to dabble in crypto currency in the words of Kavita Gupta of Delta Blockchain Fund.

"A student from a village in Punjab studying engineering and working as a receptionist had crypto money. She invested ₹100 everyday in crypto from the salary that she earned as a receptionist. Later she earned so much money through crypto that she was able to pay her education loan. So as far as digitalisation of financial services are concerned, options for investments and savings have dimensionally increased and become easier and young girls are willingly experimenting."

Gupta notes that though investing in crypto involves risks, a large chunk of the investors are women. "Young people think about crypto currency as a global currency." Stating the second reason she says, "Investing in crypto allows privacy to women. They don't have to share their currency with anyone or give it away in marriage."

Whatever the instrument of investment, and whatever the ups and downs, if the concepts are made simpler and more commonplace, women will find money matters less intimidating. "Making bank accounts, handling money online and accessing other financial services should be as simple as using WhatsApp and TikTok." She also says, "Fintech should consider two groups of women, one who are between 18 to 35, who are ambitious, have smartphones and are digital savvy, and other who are beyond 35, have to take care of family and are not very familiar with the digital world."

I really believe women should be financially independent from men. Money gives men the power to run the show and define what's okay, what's not, what drives the world, and what the big ideas are. This needs to change.

One of the big reasons we feel alone in our journey with money is because we don't know who to talk to, or if we should talk to someone at all. We don't realise that our best friend sitting across from us in the coffee shop is going through something similar. We fear being judged and called money-minded.

A few months ago, when I was busy meeting venture capitalists for a project, a few women told me how they went to raise money with a sense of apology for trying something new or an idea that had not been done before. Interestingly, men who went with a new concept, with no other example in the market to back it, would sell it brilliantly and ask for three times more than the women because they "were creating the idea". One survey went to the extent of saying nearly 80% of women interviewed preferred to have a male co-founder "just so they could raise more money". Cliched as this falls on your ears, it's the truth. The small percentage of women who are raising well, and in a gender-agnostic way, should not deter us from believing and understanding the deep-rooted problem. "Women should be trained to talk about money because we are conditioned to not talk about it," says Yashasvi Vaid, who is building a business in eco-friendly bags.

It's also interesting how money links to so many other things women must invest in. Bhavna Toor of *Shenomics* has a three-point agenda on this—self-awareness, courageous mindset, and visibility. "Cultivating an understanding of what is important to you, what drives you, your values, what you are good at and can get better at, what is a vision that is most exciting to you, as well as an awareness of how others see you."

Growing up, I was always taught to speak up for myself. It wasn't until I got older that I realised not everyone received the same lesson. If you want something, ask for it—because no one is going to give it to you otherwise. I once shocked my editor when I walked into his cabin and told him I needed a two-time raise because I totally deserve it. And I got it. Women are less likely to ask for a raise compared to their male counterparts. Talking about money with other women helps to not only foster a healthy sisterhood with the subject, but it can also encourage us to ask for what we are worth.

The good news is that young women are now asking for more, raising their hand, and depending a little more on each other to have the sisterhood lift them up each time they fall.

chapter fourteen

The Power of the Sisterhood

Sometime in the late 2000s, I was just two days into my new job and seeing how headstrong I was, my managing editor slipped in a threat casually, "You'll never be able to take my chair." I was always aware that the senior positions in news agencies are male-dominated but utterly shocked that people were able to verbalise it openly. Without a moment of hesitation, I retorted—"Who wants your cabin? I'll be CEO someday."

Growing up, I was used to people telling me that I'm way too ambitious. My parents always encouraged lunch time arguments—we spoke about society, women, politics, and literally everything under the sun. No surprise that since the age of eight, I knew that I wanted to be a news reader and reporter. Because of my liberal family set-up, I had the courage to call out a wrong when I saw one. As an 11-year-old, I confronted an elder relative who told my mother that "working in television is no different than being a prostitute".

I bluntly said—"You are wrong" and told my parents that I never wanted to see him again.

I worked as a reporter for over 20 years and in 2015, when digital media was gaining prominence, I knew that it was time to act. There was not a single platform that dealt with the real issues faced by women. I was sure that I wanted to do something about this and discussed it with my husband—"Can I run my own channel?" and he said—"Why not?" At the peak of my prime time career, I decided to quit my job and took a leap of faith with *SheThePeople*. It was India's first digital platform dedicated to women and the real issues faced by them—be it skin shaming, mansplaining, or breaking traditional gender stereotypes. From inspiring stories to talking about taboo issues, we do it all.

A lot of people discouraged me—"Are you sure you can do it alone?", "Who would want to follow a channel that is only about women?" Although I was determined, it was not easy at all. I used to doubt myself every few days, and I questioned my plan to build a women-focussed platform so many times.

Just the other day I asked myself, what's the one thing I would like to have had back then, that might have helped me take the leap of faith without fear? The answer was a sisterhood. There is nothing more inspirational than another determined woman around you, encouraging you to take the plunge. For some of us there is encouragement at home, in an odd friend, but often what's absent is the network.

A sisterhood can create strong connections that last forever, whilst also bringing a sense of belonging to people who might feel isolated and alone. Having a sense of belonging is so important to all women and girls, and the acceptance from the group can help individuals show acceptance and growth within themselves. I often say that behind every woman is herself but there is something to be said of a larger community that backs each other.

We need more women to champion each other and break that trope that a woman is a woman's worst enemy. I read this somewhere and it remains very powerful. "Surround yourself with women who will take your name in a room full of opportunities." This is important and it changes the game.

Most of us are equipped to guide and advise, many times we don't do that. Maybe we don't pay too much attention to this, or just decide to overlook it. Something just holds us back from stepping in to save a day for someone. I feel that we don't need to do that. We need to rise above our insecurities, our jealousies, and be there for each other, whenever, whatever the circumstances.

It is a fact that not every one of us is born confident. It is also a fact that life constantly puts us to test, presenting us with situations and circumstances that are not only not in our control but many times unexpected, uncalled for, and even frightening. What is more, as women most of the times we are expected to not only have solutions to a problem, but are also expected to put on that brave face and pretend that all is in control, when actually nothing is. That may make the task even more daunting and at times almost impossible.

Everyone needs that network in their lives that can

just take them in with no questions asked and accept them for who they are.

Today, my platform has completed seven years—we have a digital reach of over one billion a year. I spend a great deal of my time talking with women about their challenges and how I can help them. I took a chance on myself and yes, I am a kickass CEO and I am self made—all of that has built me into a mean machine who is her own champion. And so it's my duty to pass that on and pay it forward. That's sisterhood for me.

Men Can Play a Role

Sometime ago I was invited to speak with Stanford law students who were on a field trip to India. In the room were about 12 men, and my professor Erik Jenson asked me to reflect on inequalities in India and leave a parting message. Even for the most seasoned talkers, putting together an impromptu message to a room full of intellectuals can be tough.

And so I turned to them, and said, "The biggest solution for inequality in our country lies with you all. The men in front of me." Suddenly I had all their attention. "Men can turn the stereotype switch off in the minds of other men with a lot more ease, and friendly banter than even a small comment or speech by a woman. I urge you today, to think of why this ask of equality needs to be tedious to work upon. Why is it a woman's problem? We can only fix this world together. And I believe, as a woman, I need men to become my problem solvers too." To this, one of the students turned back—and this was I think 2019, late in the year—and said, "I never thought of it as my responsibility."

I thought my work was done. I had made a most important point to men, to whom their role in gender equality efforts was not even understood. When I see Farhan Akhtar champion MARD or Ranveer Singh come out and speak up in awe of his wife's work ethic or just notice how George Clooney reminds us that Amal is a Khan before Clooney—these are signs and big signals of how public discourse should be. To some, such things look trivial, but there will be unsung heroes working in the trenches, villages, and shaping the new global agenda of an equal world. But we will by all means need the next big TikToker, the Bollywood hero, or villain to come out and say it like it is.

Here's another personal experience from when I went over to meet the Indian women's hockey team upon their arrival from the Olympics. A news reporter was talking to a young champion from our female hockey team named Neha Goyal. When the reporter saw India's goalkeeper Sreejesh—who had become a hero of sorts—he dropped Neha's interview midway and ran after Sreejesh. "What's wrong with you? How can you stop this interview midway?" I asked the reporter. And before I knew it, Sreejesh came right there and said to this young man, "How can you be so disrespectful and leave an interview in the middle?" Whether its films or fintech, men are leading every sector and so their influence in changing the conversation about women can be useful fuel to our efforts.

Conclusion

When I set out to write *Sisterhood Economy*, I didn't want to strap a bunch of graphs and data points on women or suggest that understanding "economy" was reserved for those who saw it only in terms of numbers. To me, it's about people. An economy and what it offers people ought to be pretty simple and be about details we tend to miss out on. Like Ludia working at home to fund her daughter's nursing course so she never has to sweep houses. Mohua selling masala (curry patta, ginger, and garlic in a small one-time portion) because earning her own money is important to her. Chinamma buying fish from the wholesaler to sell in her town at a profit so she can get her granddaughter a fresh string of mallipu (jasmine flowers). Aamna building her fashion blog so she can buy her own apartment and help her parents live debt free. At the core, we know economy isn't the math of buying and selling—it's about what people derive from it. It's about what you can share and what you can trigger. It's an extract of our fightback and our desires and everything that comes in its way.

When comedian Mallika Dua and I talk about why

women are expected to be likeable, we are taking note of how it has an economic impact and deters women from speaking up and asking for their rightful spaces. When Byju's co-founder, Divya Gokulnath, reminds us that buying your own diamonds is better than your husband buying them, she is firing up a belief in those who are yet to find it. The day Malti didi left her abusive husband and found a job in the city, she was frightened, but it changed her economics and made her fearless. You see where I am going. Numbers are important—less than a quarter of Indian women go to work, 20 die every day because of dowry demands, every four minutes a woman is diagnosed with breast cancer—and they must guide to more material fixes for ourselves and society. What we need to do, more than ever, is to move beyond the statistics and wheedle a new sensibility where girls and women flourish, get equal opportunities, and break traditions that hold us back.

I am driven by purpose and that comes from a deep sense of seeing change. Whether it's about building *Gytree* as the next big frontier for women's health in India or establishing *SheThePeople* as a voice for women across the world. I remain staggered with the responsibilities I share with millions of other women to be the change we want to see. Growing up as two sisters in a simple household, I had dreams that seemed so impractical at the time. Never did I think I would build and run institutions, but I did. And so, I say this to all women and girls out there, don't hone your dreams into what's possible but dream of what's not, and go for it.

"You are too young to achieve that." As someone who was editing a channel's primetime news in her

20s, this is a phrase I heard a lot. And it came from outsiders, "wellwishers", and even friends. They said they were protecting me from a vicious environment that didn't believe in young, ambitious women wanting more. I didn't agree with them, but it wasn't their fault—they didn't know better. Now we do. We must support women and girls who are steering a new course that makes society uncomfortable and makes them rewire. We should stop looking at women as baby bearers, multitaskers, superwomen, and givers of all and start celebrating them as individuals who rise, fall, grow, cry, succeed, struggle, and remain real. We need to put a new triptych in place—awareness, access, and availability of opportunity—no matter what age or how they identify themselves.

How we report and write about women will also amend perceptions. Remember when Abhijit Banerjee and Esther Duflo won the Nobel Prize for Economics? A newspaper in India reported that "Abhijit Banerjee and his wife won the prize." No reference was made to Duflo as an economist, or the third person who won the award, Michael Kramer. Duflo is an acclaimed economist in her own right and the youngest person ever to win a Nobel Prize, besides being the second woman to win it for economics.

It's routine for us to talk about social media likes and hearts for men, on their household achievements strewn across TikTok and Instagram. But read this. Do these sound stupid when women say it? *Definitely allowing my husband to work after marriage. I help my husband with household chores. Where is my "wife of the year" award? I allow my partner to wear whatever the hell that he wants. I will be totally cool about my husband wanting to keep his surname after marriage. Am okay with my husband earning more than me, I am a cool wife. I want my husband to be a stay-at-home dad so someone can take care of the children while I work and earn money for my family.*

It's ironic but amazingly true how a social media post can change how we think. It seeds a little atom and exposes us to a fast-growing sisterhood that we have not even met in flesh and blood. Every day in my DMs, we get messages from young women and men sharing how they are contesting and questioning the stereotypical status-quo. A conversation has begun and is having an impact. Transgressions that probe patriarchy are not always noisy—many are silent, but no less fierce.

While we seek a remodelling of the social construct around us, as girls and women, let's not wear armoured suits and be Rambo. I was raised to hold back, hide, and abstain from expressing vulnerabilities. Part of building a sisterhood economy is to have it on one's own terms and that includes openness. I recently became an Aspen Fellow and one thing from my conversations there stayed with me—how being vulnerable makes us relevant as people and makes us authentic. So, as I conclude this book, I urge you to ask yourself some questions and not fear being judged.

Whose life am I living? Am I dreaming enough? Am I asking for help when I need it? What's my calling? How can I support her?

I often say, behind every woman is herself, but truly, if the sisterhood powers her journey, we will be stronger together and drive serious economic outcomes.

References

Someone said learning to write is always part of reading. And in my case, that's always been true. I am a voracious reader and find so much inspiration in powerful writing around me. Here are a few of the books that inspired me when I was writing:

All the Single Ladies: Unmarried Women and the Rise of an Independent Nation, Rebecca Traister, Simon and Schuster, 2016

Invisible Women: Exposing Data Bias in a World Designed for Men, Caroline Criado Perez, Vintage Books, 2020

May You Be the Mother of a Hundred Sons, Elizabeth Bumiller, Penguin India, 2000

My Life in Full: Work, Family and Our Future, Indra Nooyi, Hachette India, 2021

Caste: The Lies that Divide Us, Isabel Wilkerson, Allen Lane, 2020

A Room of One's Own, Virginia Woolf, Penguin Classics, 2019

My Own Words, Ruth Bader Ginsburg with Mary Hartnett and Wendy W Williams, Simon and Schuster, Reprint, 2018

Hello Mum, Polly Dunbar, Faber and Faber, 2021

Women in the Indian Economy, edited by VS Ganesamurthy, New Century Publications, 2008

Rage Becomes Her, Soraya Chemaly, Atria Books, 2018

Unladylike: A Memoir, Radhika Vaz, Aleph Book Company, 2015

I read the works of cartoonist and illustrator Liza Donnelly, whose works are caustic and sharp, about how society treats women. I picked up *Economic and Policy Weekly*, after decades (it was required reading in college I remember) and feasted on specific papers.

I also went through copious amounts of footage from *SheThePeople*'s archives and looked at what's shaping the narratives in the lives of the many women we interview. My earlier books *When I Was 25* and *Feminist Rani*, still widely read, were also good sources of information on what drives women to seek freedom.

Acknowledgements

Writing this book has been an emotional experience, along with a journey of learning, and I am thankful to the many people who supported me. I am a sucker for inspiration, and I was determined to find a bit of many different people's stories and gain from their lived moments.

I am no economist. I am a journalist-turned-entrepreneur and it's that nuanced, imperfect, and practical understanding of my world that led to the birth of *Sisterhood Economy*. The chaotic lives of women and every other mess that drives their everyday successes and struggles were critical inputs into the book that this has become.

I would like to thank my editor, Himanjali Sankar, for her ardent belief in this idea and the patience she has shown through the unexpected years of the pandemic that pushed our book back but also gave us time to contextualise how COVID-19 pivots things for women. Also, a big thanks to Mridu Agarwal for the cover and Megha Mukherjee for proofreading this book and loving it.

From among my colleagues, I would like to mention Rudrani Gupta for being researcher for a large part of this book despite her demanding health, Yamini Pustake, the ideas editor at *SheThePeople* for being a nuanced reviewer of some of my chapters, Smita Singh for sharing under-the-skin stories, Deepshikha Chakravarti for driving *SheThePeople* and giving me time and space to find my book's central calling. Also, would like to mention Charvi Kathuria, Hemant Chandiramani, and Ratan Priya for all their support.

There's a saying: surround yourself with women and men who will call your name in a room full of opportunities. I have so many such people to thank who directly or indirectly, triggered in me a new goal, new energies and pushed me to do more. I am thankful for all the mentorship and inspiration I have had from industrialist Anand Mahindra.

The idea of the book was seeded in the corridors of Stanford's Encina Hall where I was present for a fellowship in the Centre of Democracy, Development and Rule of Law, and to that extent, I have to thank Francis Fukuyama and Erik Jenson for the many formal and informal conversations on gender and democracy. A special mention for development economist Vijendra Rao, who is also a friend, and very early in my book journey, guided me to books and research that focused on women.

I was inspired through the course of my writing by reading the many authors I did. You can find a big and very credible list in the inspirations section of this book.

This book's acknowledgements cannot be complete

without me thanking the communities of *SheThePeople* and *Girl Talk India* across the world. The hundreds of DMs I get about stereotypes women live with, the truth bombs they share, and the questions they want raised. These gave me the guts to question, for example, mothers and mothers-in-law alike and share many other stories fearlessly.

I would like to thank my family for being patient with my working hours with no weekends and vacations, because, as many of you know, books happen with the rest of work going on as usual. My husband, Shivnath, an economist by training, was a fantastic sounding board to the anecdotal notions I present. My parents raised me as a vociferous, fierce, and independent woman and am thankful for that because without such an upbringing I wouldn't even be thinking of writing this book. My dad-in-law has been the baby-sitter-in-chief of my kids since they were born, and I'm very thankful for that. My sister and her husband are both entrepreneurs and have been an inspiration for me to break new barriers. I have to thank Noor and Ajmeera, the two women who run and support my household and supplied me with endless cups of loose-leaf chai during the course of this book. I can't not thank my kids, Abeer and Bani, for being so little and yet so understanding of my commitments and time. Bani once drew me on her slate, as a woman with her laptop and wine glass. It's the most accurate portrait someone can make of me.

And lastly, funny as it sounds, I am learning from the very women and girls we talk with—that one must acknowledge oneself. So, I am thankful to myself. For wanting to write this book, for taking it away from just being an idea in the universe to putting it down on paper, for being vulnerable with remarkable sang froid, for sharing honestly my personal experiences and journeys, and for being me.

About the Author

Shaili Chopra is a gamechanger in India's content landscape, having brought women's issues to the forefront like none other and creating a path-breaking digital platform like SheThePeople.TV with a reach of 400 million. She has to her credit key global fellowships like the Draper Hills Fellowship from Stanford University and Vital Voices. Shaili is a recipient of India's biggest journalism award, the Ramnath Goenka Award for Journalism. She has authored five books.

By creating a platform like SheThePeople, with real stories of real women, Shaili has been named among the top 50 women in media and marketing who are changing the democratic fabric of India by putting women's voices on the policy tables. Shaili is currently building a new initiative that puts women's health at the centre of making women the next powerhouse for the Indian economy.